D0079927

Not for Profit. All for Education.

Oxford University Press USA is a not-for-profit publisher dedicated to offering the highest quality textbooks at the best possible prices. We believe that it is important to provide everyone with access to superior textbooks at affordable prices. Oxford University Press textbooks are 30%–70% less expensive than comparable books from commercial publishers.

The press is a department of the University of Oxford, and our publishing proudly serves the university's mission: promoting excellence in research, scholarship, and education around the globe. We do not publish in order to generate revenue: we generate revenue in order to publish and also to fund scholarships, provide start-up grants to early-stage researchers, and refurbish libraries.

What does this mean to you? It means that Oxford University Press USA published this book to best support your studies while also being mindful of your wallet.

Not for Profit. *All* for Education.
As a not-for-profit publisher, Oxford University Press USA is uniquely situated to offer the highest quality scholarship at the best possible prices.

OXFORD
UNIVERSITY PRESS

READING AMERICAN HORIZONS

READING AMERICAN HORIZONS

PRIMARY SOURCES FOR U.S. HISTORY IN A GLOBAL CONTEXT
VOLUME I: TO 1877

THIRD EDITION

Michael Schaller
UNIVERSITY OF ARIZONA

Janette Thomas Greenwood
CLARK UNIVERSITY

Andrew Kirk
UNIVERSITY OF NEVADA, LAS VEGAS

Sarah J. Purcell
GRINNELL COLLEGE

Aaron Sheehan-Dean
LOUISIANA STATE UNIVERSITY

Christina Snyder
PENNSYLVANIA STATE UNIVERSITY

With contributions by:

Robert Schulzinger
UNIVERSITY OF COLORADO, BOULDER

John Bezís-Selfa
WHEATON COLLEGE

Oxford University Press is a department of the University of Oxford. It furthers the University's objective of excellence in research, scholarship, and education by publishing worldwide. Oxford is a registered trade mark of Oxford University Press in the UK and certain other countries.

Published in the United States of America by Oxford University Press
198 Madison Avenue, New York, NY 10016, United States of America.

Library of Congress Cataloging-in-Publication Data

Names: Schaller, Michael, 1947- author.
Title: Reading American horizons : primary sources for U.S. history in a
  global context / Michael Schaller, University of Arizona ... [and seven others].
Other titles: Primary sources for U.S. history in a global context
Description: Third edition. | New York, NY : Oxford University Press, [2018]
Identifiers: LCCN 2017016876| ISBN 9780190698034 (pbk. volume 1) |
  ISBN 9780190698041 (pbk. volume 2)
Subjects: LCSH: United States—History.
Classification: LCC E178 .A5527 2018 | DDC 973—dc23
LC record available at https://lccn.loc.gov/2017016876

CONTENTS

PREFACE

Reading American Horizons is a primary source reader for the survey course in American history, designed to accompany the textbook *American Horizons*.

For more than four hundred years, North America has been part of a global network centered upon the exchange of peoples, goods, and ideas. Human migrations—sometimes freely, sometimes forced—have continued over the centuries, along with the evolution of commerce in commodities as varied as tobacco, sugar, and computer chips. Europeans and Africans came or were brought to the continent, where they met, traded with, fought among, and intermarried with native peoples. Some of these migrants stayed, while others returned to their home countries. Still others came and went periodically. This initial circulation of people across the oceans foreshadowed the continuous movement of people, goods, and ideas that forged the United States. These forces shaped American history, both dividing and unifying the nation. American "horizons" truly stretch beyond our nation's borders, embracing the trading networks established during and after the colonial era to the digital social networks connecting people globally today.

Reading American Horizons uses primary source materials to help tell the story of the United States by exploring this exchange on a global scale and placing it at the center of that story. By doing so, we provide a different perspective on the history of the United States, one that we hope broadens the horizons of those who read our work and are ever mindful of the global forces that increasingly and profoundly shape our lives. At the same time, *Reading American Horizons* considers those ways in which U.S. influence reshaped the lives and experiences of people of other nations.

Understanding documents and visual artifacts from the past is vital to the study of history. *Reading American Horizons* presents a selection of these materials, all carefully selected to complement the narrative and themes presented in the accompanying *American Horizons*. It is our intention that students more deeply understand the historical narrative in the textbook by examining the original sources in this reader, and that the contextual introductions and review questions enrich the interpretations we offer in the textbook.

How did the United States emerge from a diverse set of colonies? How did colonists interact with Native American nations? How did the United States become a major player on the world stage of nations? What qualities make the United States unique? What does the United States share with other nations and empires? History includes many storylines that contribute to this narrative. *Reading American Horizons* provides insight into the story of where this nation came from and how it has been shaped by its own set of shared values as well as its interaction with the rest of the world. *Reading American Horizons* depicts the intersection of storylines from many nations that influenced, and were influenced by, the United States of America.

As readers engage these materials, we encourage them to think explicitly about what makes history. What matters? What forces or events shaped how people lived their lives? What types of sources do historians rely on to explain the past? With all the sources in this book, readers should consider both what the creators hoped to accomplish and how people at the time might have read or viewed them. We encourage you to become your own historian, to read, analyze, and imagine the connections among the different voices that helped make the United States.

THE DEVELOPMENT STORY

The six co-editors of this book specialize in a variety of time periods and methodologies. Based on our research and teaching, we all share the idea that the nation's history can best be understood by examining how, from the precolonial era forward, the American experience reflected the interaction of many nations, peoples, and events. We present this idea in a format that integrates traditional narrative history with the enhanced perspective of five centuries of global interaction.

CHANGES TO THIS EDITION

In this edition, we are happy to welcome a new co-editor, Christina Snyder, who revitalized the first five chapters with nine new primary sources that reflect the most recent scholarship of America's history in a global context before 1763. In addition, four new sources have been added to chapters 6–15.

CHAPTER 1:

- Swimmer as told to James Mooney, "Origin of Disease and Medicine," (1880s and undated oral traditions)
- Letters from Afonso, King of Kongo, to João III, King of Portugal (1526)
- Rodrigo Rangel, "Account of the Northern Conquest and Discovery of Hernando de Soto" (1540)

CHAPTER 2:

- Richard Hakluyt, Excerpts from "A Brief Relation of Two Sundry Voyages" (1598)
- Jacques Gravier's Account of the Marriage of Marie Rouensa (1694)

CHAPTER 1

THE ORIGINS OF THE ATLANTIC WORLD, ANCIENT TIMES TO 1565

1.1. SWIMMER AS TOLD TO JAMES MOONEY, "ORIGIN OF DISEASE AND MEDICINE," (1880s AND UNDATED ORAL TRADITIONS)

Even before the arrival of Europeans, Native Americans dealt with disease. They had developed theories about the origin of disease as well as medicinal practices for coping with disease. The following oral tradition comes from Ayunini, a Cherokee whose name means "Swimmer." Trained in traditional ways, Swimmer was a Cherokee priest, doctor, and storyteller. He was particularly accomplished in botanical medicine; this oral tradition helps explain why. The anthropologist James Mooney recorded this story in the late 1880s, but its origins are much older, for Swimmer preserved the ancient lore of his people.

In the old days the beasts, birds, fishes, insects, and plants could all talk, and they and the people lived together in peace and friendship. But as time went on the people increased so rapidly that their settlements spread over the whole earth, and the poor animals found themselves beginning to be cramped for room. This was bad enough, but to make it worse Man invented bows, knives, blowguns, spears, and hooks, and began to slaughter the larger animals, birds, and fishes for their flesh or their skins, while the smaller creatures, such as the frogs and worms, were crushed and trodden upon without thought, out of pure carelessness or contempt. So the animals resolved to consult upon measures for their common safety.

The Bears were the first to meet in council in their townhouse under Kuwâ'hï mountain, the "Mulberry place," and the old White Bear chief presided. After each in turn had complained of the way in which Man killed their friends, ate their flesh, and used their skins for his own purposes, it was decided to begin war at once against him. Some one asked what weapons Man used to destroy them. "Bows and arrows, of course," cried all the Bears in chorus. "And what are they made of?" was the next question. "The bow of wood, and the

Source: James Mooney, "Myths of the Cherokee," in *Nineteenth Annual Report of the Bureau of American Ethnology 1897–1898* (Washington, D.C.: U.S. Government Printing Office, 1900), Part 1, 250–252.

string of our entrails," replied one of the Bears. It was then proposed that they make a bow and some arrows and see if they could not use the same weapons against Man himself. So one Bear got a nice piece of locust wood and another sacrificed himself for the good of the rest in order to furnish a piece of his entrails for the string. But when everything was ready and the first Bear stepped up to make the trial, it was found that in letting the arrow fly after drawing back the bow, his long claws caught the string and spoiled the shot. This was annoying, but someone suggested that they might trim his claws, which was accordingly done, and on a second trial it was found that the arrow went straight to the mark. But here the chief, the old White Bear, objected, saying it was necessary that they should have long claws in order to be able to climb trees. "One of us has already died to furnish the bowstring, and if we now cut off our claws we must all starve together. It is better to trust to the teeth and claws that nature gave us, for it is plain that man's weapons were not intended for us."

No one could think of any better plan, so the old chief dismissed the council and the Bears dispersed to the woods and thickets without having concerted any way to prevent the increase of the human race. Had the result of the council been otherwise, we should now be at war with the Bears, but as it is, the hunter does not even ask the Bear's pardon when he kills one.

The Deer next held a council under their chief, the Little Deer, and after some talk decided to send rheumatism to every hunter who should kill one of them unless he took care to ask their pardon for the offense. They sent notice of their decision to the nearest settlement of Indians and told them at the same time what to do when necessity forced them to kill one of the Deer tribe. Now, whenever the hunter shoots a Deer, the Little Deer, who is swift as the wind and cannot be wounded, runs quickly up to the spot and, bending over the blood-stains, asks the spirit of the Deer if it has heard the prayer of the hunter for pardon. If the reply be "Yes," all is well, and the Little Deer goes on his way; but if the reply be "No," he follows on the trail of the hunter, guided by the drops of blood on the ground, until he arrives at his cabin in the settlement, when the Little Deer enters invisibly and strikes the hunter with rheumatism, so that he becomes at once a helpless cripple. No hunter who has regard for his health ever fails to ask pardon of the Deer for killing it, although some hunters who have not learned the prayer may try to turn aside the Little Deer from his pursuit by building a fire behind them in the trail.

. . . Finally the Birds, Insects, and smaller animals came together for the same purpose, and the Grubworm was chief of the council. It was decided that each in turn should give an opinion, and then they would vote on the question as to whether or not Man was guilty. Seven votes should be enough to condemn him. One after another denounced Man's cruelty and injustice toward the other animals and voted in favor of his death. The Frog spoke first, saying: "We must do something to check the increase of the race, or people will become so numerous that we shall be crowded from off the earth. See how they have kicked me about because I'm ugly, as they say, until my back is covered with sores"; and here he showed the spots on his skin. Next came the Bird—no one remembers now which one it was—who condemned Man "because he burns my feet off," meaning the way in which the hunter barbecues birds by impaling them on a stick set over the fire, so that their feathers and tender feet are singed off. Others followed in the same strain. . . .

They began then to devise and name so many new diseases, one after another, that had not their invention at last failed them, no one of the human race would have been able to survive. The Grubworm grew constantly more pleased as the name of each disease was called off, until at last they reached the end of the list, when someone proposed to make menstruation sometimes fatal to women. On this he rose up in his place and cried: "*Wadâñ'!* [Thanks!] I'm glad some more of them will die, for they are getting so thick that they tread on me." The thought fairly made him shake with joy, so that he fell over backward and could not get on his feet again, but had to wriggle off on his back, as the Grubworm has done ever since.

When the Plants, who were friendly to Man, heard what had been done by the animals, they determined to defeat the latter's evil designs. Each Tree, Shrub, and Herb, down even to the Grasses and Mosses, agreed to furnish a cure for some one of the diseases named, and each said: "I shall appear to help Man when he calls upon me in his need." Thus came medicine; and the plants, every one of which has its use if we only knew it, furnish the remedy to counteract the evil wrought by the revengeful animals. Even weeds were made for some good purpose, which we must find out for ourselves. When the doctor does not know what medicine to use for a sick man the spirit of the plant tells him.

QUESTIONS

1. What does this story suggest about humans' role in the world?

2. Oral traditions offer a window into a people's worldview and value system. What does this story attempt to teach the listener?

3. In the colonial era, Euro-Americans held varied beliefs about disease and medicine; some of them overlapped with Native beliefs and some did not. However, many Euro-Americans sought out Indian doctors and cures. Why?

1.2. FERNANDO AND JUANA, MONARCHS OF CASTILE AND ARAGON (SPAIN), "INSTRUCTIONS GIVEN BY THE MONARCHS TO RODRIGO DE ALBURQUERQUE AND TO LICENTIATE IBARRA TO BE CARRIED OUT DURING THE GENERAL DISTRIBUTION OF THE INDIANS IN THE ISLAND OF HISPANIOLA," EXCERPTS (1513)

By 1512, outcries from missionaries and other reports from Española had alerted royal officials in Spain that conquest and colonization had decimated the island's Taíno peoples. Although imperial officials enacted some reforms intended to protect Taínos, they also knew and had to acknowledge that Española's economy and royal revenues from the island depended on compulsory Taíno labor. The following document contains excerpts from royal orders issued in 1513 to two officials conducting a *repartimiento*, an allocation of Taíno labor on the island among towns and individual colonists, a task that in effect required that they compile a census of Española's Indians. Officials hoped that the repartimiento and other reforms would help to stem the decline of the Taínos while protecting Spain's economic ventures in Española.

Source: The Dominican People: A Documentary History. Eds. Ernesto Sagás and Orlando Inoa. (Princeton: Markus Wiener Publishers, 2003), 17–23. This document was translated from Luis Arranz Márquez, *Repartimientos y encomiendas en la Isla Española: El Repartimiento de Alburquerque de 1514* (Santo Domingo: Fundación García Arévalo, 1991): 263–73.

This copy was faithfully transcribed from a decree given by the King.

The King: What you, Licentiate Ibarra and Rodrigo de Alburquerque, must do, in your position of *enco-mendador*[1] of the Indians, so that, according to the lettered men's[2] resolution, they would be treated and indoctrinated in Our Holy Catholic Faith is to abide by the following: . . .

2. Second, by the virtue of the decree you carry, you shall revoke and annul, through a public announcement, the current Allocations of the Indians, this is, as determined by our erudite men, in order to cleanse our conscience. And you should order that everyone, including our officials, anyone under our name, the Admiral[3] and his wife, the appellate judges, as well as our officers and all the people, of every class and condition, report each of the Indians they possess, and the name of the caciques[4] under whose command they are, and the name of each Indian, be it men or women, boys or girls, to the Indian Visitor and a delegate, who will be elected in every town for such, and other, purposes. . . .

4. And then, you should order each of the town mayors to visit, within a twenty-day period, the Indians in the neighboring farms and ask their caciques for a list of names and allocation of each of their Indians. The lists should be sent to you by the mayors within a reasonable period of time.

5. And then, you should order that a record of all the people that live in each town should be created under the supervision of the mayor and the secretary of each town. And these records should be signed by the mayor and the secretary and brought to you by the delegate, as well as the list of the declared Indians, and a report of the visit that the mayors paid to each of the caciques.

. . . 7. Completed this first part of the task, what you shall do next is to see that the general distribution of the Indians is just, according to its population, so that no town is affected by having fewer Indians. At the same time, you should consider if a town has been allocated too many Indians in respect to its population. This is so that no one feels the need to present a protest as in the village of Puerto Real where people were affected. They say they have very few, and extremely necessary Indians, who are very useful in the trade with Cuba. Make sure that no other town, but the one already mentioned, is affected. . . . The Indians should stay in their original places to avoid the inconveniences of moving them around. But if a general redistribution of Indians is necessary, make sure you privilege those communities that have mines in them, because they will be more useful to us.

. . . 9. [Having] completed the general Allocation, and if changes must be made in order to meet the needs of each town, and if nothing else needs to be done, then you should proceed to make the individual distributions.

10. In this matter, the first thing to be considered, . . . is that no Indian shall be allocated in two places at the same time. This is because by their [the Indians] being in several places, the control as to their instruction and doctrine in our sacred Catholic faith and in the communication with Christians as to their good treatment, in the hands of the people who have them, cannot be clearly maintained. . . .

12. And because it has been called to our attention that the number of Indians in the island has been declining, and at the same time, some people have too many of them and cannot, therefore, indoctrinate them and teach them the tenets of Our Holy Faith nor can they all be well treated, as reasonable, and because more can now communicate in Christian, and in order to expedite their individual allocations, we mandate that you adhere to the instructions, following the number of Indians allocated without exceeding them.

13. In our Haciendas you may leave the number of Indians that are now there, as long as that number does not exceed one thousand. The Admiral shall keep three hundred and his wife, María de Toledo, two hundred Indians. To the people who serve me but are not in the island, who are: the First Chaplain of my Council, the

---

1. A good rough translation would be "caretaker."
2. Theologians of the Spanish royal court, charged with advising monarchs on the morality of proposed laws and policies.
3. Diego Columbus, Christopher's son.
4. Taíno chiefs.

Reverend in Christ Father Don Juan Fonseca, Bishop of Palencia, shall receive two hundred Indians; Fernando Vega, Comendador Mayor of Castile, two hundred; Chamberlain Juan Cabrero, two hundred; Secretary Lope Conchillos, two hundred; to the judges, officers, mayors, I order each shall receive two hundred; and to the descendants of the Admiral and their uncles two hundred Indians each.

14. The rest of the people who live in the island to whom you shall allocate Indians, should be divided within four groups as follows: The most honorable and respectful people, among which you will surely find my servants Villoria and Porros amongst others, should receive the largest possible number of Indians which will be of one hundred and fifty.

15. The second group will be of one hundred Indians and those would be allocated to the next following honorable people you hear of.

16. The third group shall receive seventy-five Indians.

17. The last group shall receive forty Indians, and the rest of the people shall receive none because I understand that less than forty are of no use, and of no profit because those who have them would not bring the one-third profit that was established in the ordinance.

18. And also, because we have been informed that many people have ten or fewer Indians and for this small number we receive no profit. So we order that you collect those Indians from the people that only have three, four, or six and up to ten, so that they may be relocated, especially the Indian men. But the Indian women can stay because many of them are used as house servants and maids, and they shall be indoctrinated and taught in the house. This is so long as they are not married, because according to the Lettered Men, the married women and the children under thirteen years of age must do as the Indian man orders, for they are subjected to his will. If any of these Indians hold vital positions in the mines such as blacksmith or similar occupations, they should be left there.

. . . 20. And also, make sure that the Indians are not overworked as they have been until now, a matter that has caused a lot of harm and a decrease in the number of Indians. Those who have Indians, as it has been determined, shall have them use oxen to plow their land, to the extent that this could be possible, so that the Indians can preserve energy. You shall order anyone who has more than fifty Indians to obtain a pair of oxen as well to help work the land; and those people who have more than a hundred Indians shall have two pairs of oxen, and those with over two hundred should have three pairs. That is so that the more oxen they have the less overworked the Indians shall be, therefore they could serve us better, and they could have more time to be indoctrinated and to celebrate their festivities and holidays.

. . . .

Given in Valladolid, on the fourth day of October 1513.
I, the King. The Bishop of Palencia, Earl.

QUESTIONS

1. In what ways did these instructions to redistribute Indian laborers reflect and reinforce the distribution of power and wealth among colonists on Española?

2. What measures did the Spanish Crown seek to implement in order to protect Taíno lives?

3. Which of the Crown's instructions threatened to disrupt and endanger Taíno lives and how might those instructions have disrupted and endangered those lives?

1.3. LETTERS FROM AFONSO, KING OF KONGO, TO JOÃO III, KING OF PORTUGAL (1526)

The Catholic convert Afonso I assumed the throne of Kongo with Portuguese support in 1506 and ruled until 1543. Unfortunately, by the 1520s Kongo had little to pay for the imports that flooded the kingdom or provide for the Portuguese craftsmen, missionaries, arms specialists, and teachers whom Afonso invited, so they began to trade in enslaved captives, most of whom were shipped to Portuguese sugar plantations on the island of São Tomé, located off the coast of Africa. The excerpted letters that follow, originally written in Portuguese in 1526, are among the few surviving documents written by an African during the sixteenth century. Basil Davidson translated them from transcripts of the original letters printed in *História do Congo: Obra Posthuma do Visconde de Paiva Manso* (Lisbon, 1877).

[1526] Sir, Your Highness [of Portugal] should know how our Kingdom is being lost in so many ways that it is convenient to provide for the necessary remedy, since this is caused by the excessive freedom given by your factors and officials to the men and merchants who are allowed to come to this Kingdom to set up shops with goods and many things which have been prohibited by us, and which they spread throughout our Kingdoms and Domains in such an abundance that many of our vassals, whom we had in obedience, do not comply because they have the things in greater abundance than we ourselves; and it was with these things that we had them content and subjected under our vassalage and jurisdiction, so it is doing a great harm not only to the service of God, but the security and peace of our Kingdoms and State as well.

And we cannot reckon how great the damage is, since the mentioned merchants are taking every day our natives, sons of the land and the sons of our noblemen and vassals and our relatives, because the thieves and men of bad conscience grab them wishing to have the things and wares of this Kingdom which they are ambitious of; they grab them and get them to be sold; and so great, Sir, is the corruption and licentiousness that our country is being completely depopulated, and Your Highness should not agree with this nor accept it as in your service. And to avoid it we need from those [your] Kingdoms no more than some priests and a few people to teach in schools, and no other goods except wine and flour for the holy sacrament. That is why we beg of Your Highness to help and assist us in this matter, commanding your factors that they should not send here either merchants or wares, because it is *our will that in these Kingdoms there should not be any trade of slaves nor outlet for them.*[5] Concerning what is referred above, again we beg of Your Highness to agree with it, since otherwise we cannot remedy such an obvious damage. Pray Our Lord in His mercy to have Your Highness under His guard and let you do for ever the things of His service. I kiss your hands many times.

Source: Basil Davidson, *The African Past: Chronicles from Antiquity to Modern Times* (Boston: Little, Brown, 1964), 191–93. Davidson translated the letters from *História do Congo: Obra Posthuma do Visconde de Paiva Manso* (Lisbon, 1877).

5. Emphasis in the original.

At our town of Congo, written on the sixth day of July.
João Teixeira[6] did it in 1526.
The King. Dom Afonso

[*On the back of this letter the following can be read:* To the most powerful and excellent prince Dom João, King our Brother.]

THE ORIGINS OF SLAVING

[1526] Moreover, Sir, in our Kingdoms there is another great inconvenience which is of little service to God, and this is that many of our people [*naturaes*], keenly desirous as they are of the wares and things of your Kingdoms, which are brought here by your people, and in order to satisfy their voracious appetite, seize many of our people, freed and exempt men; and very often it happens that they kidnap even noblemen and the sons of noblemen, and our relatives, and take them to be sold to the white men who are in our Kingdoms; and for this purpose they have concealed them; and others are brought during the night so that they might not be recognized.

And as soon as they are taken by the white men they are immediately ironed and branded with fire, and when they are carried to be embarked, if they are caught by our guards' men the whites allege that they have bought them but they cannot say from whom, so that it is our duty to do justice and to restore to the freemen their freedom, but it cannot be done if your subjects feel offended, as they claim to be.

And to avoid such a great evil we passed a law so that any white man living in our Kingdoms and wanting to purchase goods in any way should first inform three of our noblemen and officials of our court whom we rely upon in this matter, and these are Dom Pedro Manipanza and Dom Manuel Manissaba, our chief usher, and Gonçalo Pires our chief freighter, who should investigate if the mentioned goods are captives or free men, and if cleared by them there will be no further doubt nor embargo for them to be taken and embarked. But if the white men do not comply with it they will lose the aforementioned goods. And if we do them this favor and concession it is for the part Your Highness has in it, since we know that it is in your service too that these goods are taken from our Kingdom, otherwise we should not consent to this. . . .

QUESTIONS

1. In what terms does Afonso characterize the influence of imported goods on his subjects? What does he propose that João do to regulate trade with Kongo?

2. What impact does the slave trade have on the Kongolese? What actions does Afonso take to restrict its impact?

3. In what ways did Afonso's Christian beliefs shape the message that he sent to João and what he asked of the Portuguese king?

---

6. Probably, from the evidence, a Congolese secretary educated by Portuguese missionaries at Mbanza Congo (S. Salvador). See J. Cuvelier, *L'Ancien Royaume de Congo* (Brussels: Desclée de Brouwer, 1946), 294.

1.4. RODRIGO RANGEL, "ACCOUNT OF THE NORTHERN CONQUEST AND DISCOVERY OF HERNANDO DE SOTO" (1540)

Rodrigo Rangel served as Hernando de Soto's secretary and accompanied the conquistador on his 1539–1543 expedition across the Southeast. Based on Rangel's diary, the passage below covers events that happened in 1540, though it did not appear in print until 1851. Here, Rangel describes the encounter between Hernando de Soto and the Lady of Cofitachequi, who ruled a vast chiefdom in what is now South Carolina.

[T]he Governor[7] arrived at the crossing in front of the town, and principal Indians came with gifts, and the cacica,[8] ruler of that land, came, whom the principal [Indians] brought with much prestige on a litter covered in white (with thin linen) and on their shoulders, and they crossed in the canoes, and she spoke to the Governor with much grace and self-assurance. She was young and of fine appearance, and she removed a string of pearls that she wore about the neck and put it on the Governor's neck, in order to ingratiate herself and win his good will. And all the army crossed in canoes, and they gave many presents of very well tanned hides and blankets, all very good, and a large amount of jerked venison and dry wafers, and much and very good salt. All the Indians walked covered down to the feet with very excellent hides, very well tanned, and blankets of the land. . . .

On the seventh of May, Friday, Baltasar de Gallegos[9] went with most of the people of the army to Ilapi to eat seven barbacoas[10] of corn that they said were there, which were a deposit of the cacica. This same day the Governor and Rodrigo Rangel entered in the temple or oratory of these idolatrous people, and having unwrapped some interments, they found some bodies of men tied on a barbacoa, the breasts and openings and necks and arms and legs covered in pearls. . . . They brought out from there eight or nine arrobas of pearls[11]; and as the cacica saw that the Christians made much of them, she said: "Do you think this is a lot? . . . Go to Talimeco, my town, and you will find so many that you will be unable to carry them on your horses." The governor said: "Leave them here, and to whom God gives them by good fortune, may St. Peter bless them," and so they remained. It was believed that he intended to take that [place] for himself, because without doubt it is the best that they saw and the land of better disposition, although neither many people nor much corn appeared, nor did they tarry to look for them there.

Source: John E. Worth, trans., "Account of the Northern Conquest and Discovery of Hernando do Soto by Rodrigo Rangel," in *The De Soto Chronicles: The Expedition of Hernando de Soto to North America in 1539–1543*, ed. Lawrence A. Clayton, Vernon James Knight, Jr., Edward C. Moore, 2 vols. (Tuscaloosa: University of Alabama Press, 1993), vol. 1, 278–280.

7. Hernando de Soto, who was named governor of Florida by the Spanish crown.
8. The Spanish term for a female chief. The term for male chief is cacique.
9. A captain in de Soto's army.
10. A raised platform. In this case, Rangel is speaking of a granary used to store corn.
11. One arroba is about 25 pounds, so the total is between 200 and 225 pounds.

... In the temple or oratory of Talimeco, there were breastplates, as well as corselets and helmets, made from raw and hairless hides of cows, and from the same [hides] very good shields. This Talimeco was a town of great importance, with its very authoritative oratory on a high mound; the caney or house of the cacique very large and very tall and broad, all covered, high and low, with very excellent and beautiful mats, and placed with such fine skill, that it appeared that all the mats were only one mat. Only rarely was there a hut which might not be covered with matting.

This town has very good savannahs and a fine river, and forests of walnuts and oak, pines, evergreen oaks and groves of sweetgum, and many cedars. In this river it was said that Alaminos, a native of Cuba, had found a bit of gold; and such a rumor became public in the army among the Spaniards, and for this it was believed that this is a land of gold, and that good mines would be found there.

QUESTIONS

1. What does this document reveal about the purpose of Hernando de Soto's expedition?
2. Why did the Lady of Cofitachequi encourage de Soto to visit her capital town, Talimeco?
3. Our knowledge of Mississippian culture comes primarily from archaeology, but some historical documents also provide insights into Mississippian chiefdoms, such as that of Cofitachequi. What can Rodrigo Rangel's account tell us about Mississippian culture?

1.5. VISUAL DOCUMENT: TEXAS FRAGMENT, "ARRIVAL OF CORTÉS AND MALINTZÍN IN ATLIHUETZYAN" (1530s OR 1540s)

Long before the Spanish arrived in Mexico, Nahuas (Nahuatl-speaking Indians) recorded or commemorated events and agreements by painting them in stylized ways. Shortly after central Mexico came under Spanish rule, Nahuas continued and modified this tradition to provide their own perspective on their histories, including their memories of the Spanish conquest. Artists of Tlaxcala, one of Cortés's principal allies against the Mexica, created the painting featured below. It was probably completed in the 1530s or 1540s and depicts the arrival of Cortés, Malintzín (with her hand raised to indicate that she is speaking), and a party of Spanish soldiers on horseback to Atlihuetzyan in Tlaxcala. Tepolouatecatl, a noble member of Tlaxcalan leader Xicotencatl's family, greets the visitors and offers them birds, bread, and corn, all of which are intended as tribute.

Source: Courtesy of the Nettie Lee Benson Collection of the University of Texas Library.

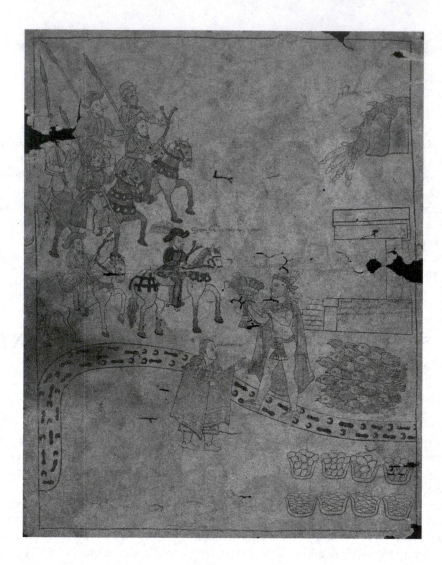

QUESTIONS

1. The road with footprints proceeding in one direction traditionally signified travel in such paintings. In what way did Tlaxcalan artists modify this sign to reflect the arrival of the Spanish?

2. Malintzín occupies a central place in this scene. Why?

3. The scene depicted here clashes with non-Tlaxcalan accounts, which indicate that many Tlaxcalan leaders decided to fight the invaders. Among the last holdouts against the Spanish was Xicotencatl's son. For what reasons did the Tlaxcalan artist(s) choose to portray the initial reception of the Spanish as peaceful?

CHAPTER 2

COLONISTS ON THE MARGINS, 1565 TO 1640

2.1. RICHARD HAKLUYT, EXCERPTS FROM "A BRIEF RELATION OF TWO SUNDRY VOYAGES" (1598)

English privateers began to trade on the Brazilian coast in the 1530s. Although Brazil was claimed by the Portuguese, who tried to monopolize trade, the English crown encouraged privateers to raid the colonies of its imperial rivals. William Hawkins was among the most famous of these privateers, trading in both West Africa and Brazil. His son, John Hawkins continued the family legacy by becoming a merchant and privateer. Both William and John Hawkins helped England become a global seafaring power. The events recorded below took place between 1530 and 1532, but they were published in 1598 by Richard Hakluyt, an Anglican minister who promoted English colonization in the Americas.

Olde M. William Haukins of Plimmouth, a man for his wisedome, valure, experience, and skill in sea causes much esteemed, and beloved of K. Henry the 8, and being one of the principall Sea captaines in the West partes of England in his time, not contented with the short voyages commonly then made onely to the knowne coasts of Europe, armed out a tall and goodly shippe of his owne of the burthen of 250 tunnes, called the Paule of Plimmouth, wherewith he made three long and famous voyages unto the coast of Brasil, a thing in those dayes very rare, especially to our Nation. In the course of which voyages he touched at the river of Sestos upon the coast of Guinea, where hee trafficqued with the Negros, and tooke of them Elephants teeth, and other commodities which that place yeeldeth: and so arriving on the coast of Brasil, he used

Source: Richard Hakluyt, "A brief relation of two sundry voyages made by the worshipful M. William Haukins [Hawkins] of Plimmouth, father to Sir John Haukins knight, late treasurer to her Majesties Navie, in the yeere 1530 and 1532," in *Principal Navigations of Voyages Traffiques and Discoveries of the English Nation*, edited by Irwin R. Blacker (New York: Viking, 1965), pp.39–40.

there such discretion, and behaved himself so wisely with those savage people, that he grew into great familiarity and friendship with them. Insomuch that in his second voyage, one of the savage kings[1] of the countrey of Brasil, was contented to take ship with him, and to be transported hither into England: whereunto M. Haukins agreed, leaving behind in the Countrey as a pledge of his safetie and returne again, one Martin Cockeram of Plimmouth. This Brasilian king being arrived, was brought up to London and presented to K. Henry the 8, lying as then at White-hall: at the sight of whom the King and all the Nobilitie did not a little marvaile, and not without cause: for in his cheeks were holes made according to their savage maner, and therein small bones were planted, standing an inch out from the said holes, which in his owne Countrey was reputed for a great braverie. He had also another hole in his nether lip, wherein was set a precious stone about the bigness of a pease[2]: All his apparel, behavior, and gesture, were very strange to the beholders.

Having remained here the space almost of a whole yeere, and the king with his sight fully satisfied, M. Hawkins [sic] according to his promise and appointment, purposed to convey him againe into his courntrey: but . . . by the change of aire and alteration of diet, the said Savage king died at sea, which was feared would turn to the losse of the life of Martin Cockeram his pledge. Nevertheless, the Savages being fully persuaded of the honest dealing of our men with their

prince, restored againe the said pledge, without any harme to him, or any man of the company: which pledge of theirs they brought home againe into England, with their ship freighted, and furnished with the commodities of the countrey. Which Martin Cockeram, by the witnesse of Sir John Hawkins, being an officer in the towne of Plimmouth, was living within these fewe yeeres.

QUESTIONS

1. Studies of this era usually focus on Europeans who traveled to Africa and the Americas, but this excerpt also demonstrates that Indigenous Americans also journeyed across the Atlantic. Thousands were slaves, but some journeyed voluntarily. Why do you think that this Brazilian chief did so? What do you think he hoped to accomplish by meeting Henry VIII and other important English political figures?

2. The early colonial period was an era of encounters when people from very different cultures met. Such encounters might forge common ground and alliance but also prejudice and conflict. How did the English respond to the Brazilian chief? How do you think the Brazilian chief might have responded to the English court?

3. Why do you think that Richard Hakluyt chose to publish this account? Why is Martin Cockeram important here?

---

1. This man was not the "king" of Brazil, but rather the chief of a region within Brazil.
2. A pea.

2.2. VISUAL DOCUMENT: SIMON VAN DE PASSE AND COMPTON HOLLAND, PORTRAIT OF POCAHONTAS (1616)

In 1616, Pocahontas, along with her husband John Rolfe, their infant son Thomas, an advisor to Powhatan named Uttamatomakin, and at least six Algonquian attendants, visited England. Officials of the struggling Virginia Company saw an opportunity to publicize the firm's work and shore up its precarious finances. They commissioned a Dutch-German artist, Simon Van de Passe, to sketch Pocahontas's portrait, from which Compton Holland made the engraving shown below. The English inscription underneath the engraving translates the Latin words that surround her image and also identifies her as a Christian convert married to John Rolfe and her father as "Emperor of Attanoughskomouck," which the English usually called Tsenacomoco. Although the engraving claims that she was 21 years old at the time of its making, she was probably only 19.

QUESTIONS

1. Pocahontas appears here in the dress of a 17th century English noblewoman. Why? Remember that the Virginia Company used this image for promotional purposes.

2. Did Pocahontas influence how Van de Passe portrayed her? What elements of the portrait and its captions suggest that she did?

3. How does this portrait differ from Pocahontas as she is depicted in film and other forms of American popular culture? Why the contrast?

Source: Virginia Historical Society, Richmond, Virginia, USA/The Bridgeman Art Library.

2.3. FRAY ALONSO DE BENAVIDES, EXCERPTS FROM "PETITION TO RESTRICT INDIAN TRIBUTE AND PERSONAL SERVICE" (c. 1630)

One of the principal sources of friction between friars and governors in Florida and New Mexico concerned the amount of tribute and personal service that Indians owed and to whom, friars or colonists, they owed that tribute and service. The friar Alonso de Benavides, who oversaw New Mexico's missions from 1626 to 1629, likely wrote the petition excerpted below. Benavides composed his petition shortly after he returned to Spain in 1630 and addressed it to the King of Spain. It appears that Benavides's efforts succeeded. In 1635, a royal decree exempted Indians in New Mexico who converted to Christianity from paying tribute or rendering personal service for ten years.

Through royal decrees it is ordered that no tributes or personal services be imposed on the Indians of New Mexico until after they have been baptized. Before any can be levied against them, the governor of the province and the custodian must notify the viceroy and the royal *audiencia*[3] of Mexico stating the reasons why they should be imposed, this to be done by the viceroy himself and the royal *audiencia*, and in no other way. At present everything is done in just the opposite manner; even before the pueblos are converted, the governor himself gives them out in *encomienda*[4] without notifying the custodian or the viceroy. Even before they are converted and baptized, when they are only pacified, they [Spaniards] constrain them to pay tribute and to do personal service, taking them far from their pueblos and treating them badly. As a result, the heathen Indians who have not yet been converted or even pacified say that they do not want to become converted, or even pacified, that they do not want to become Christians, in order not to pay tribute or serve. They have even been sent to be sold as slaves in New Spain[5], as was the practice. They escape these and other abuses as long as they remain free and do not become Christians.

Wherefore your Majesty is entreated to order, under severe penalties, that the Indians of New Mexico be not given in *encomienda* by the governors of New Mexico until five years after the whole pueblo has been baptized, and in order to be given in *encomienda*, the said governor and the custodian there must notify the viceroy and the *audiencia*, reporting that the five years have passed, so that they may be authorized to do it; that the *encomenderos*[6] of the said pueblos should have no other power or rights over the pueblos and Indians than the tribute owed them; that the Indians must remain always as tributary vassals of your Majesty, in whose name they pay the tribute to their *encomenderos*, without owing them any more obligations than to those who are not *encomenderos*; that neither the *encomenderos* nor any other Spaniards be allowed to live in their pueblos without the consent of the Indians themselves; that they may not have houses in the

Source: Frederick W. Hodge, George P. Hammond, and Agapito Rey, eds., *Fray Alonso de Benavides: Revised Memorial of 1634 with Numerous Supplementary Documents Elaborately Annotated* (Albuquerque: University of New Mexico Press, 1945), 168–77.

3. A group of judges headquartered in Mexico City who had jurisdiction over cases from New Mexico.
4. A grant to a prominent colonist of control over the services of Indians.
5. In this case, Benavides probably means what we today would call Mexico.
6. Individuals to whom a grant of *encomienda* had been given.

pueblos for their employment or other gain, by which they cause much harm to the pueblos and the Indians.

Likewise, it has been established by the first governors of New Mexico, and is being continued by order of the viceroy that each house pay a tribute consisting of a cotton blanket, the best of which are about a yard and a half square, and a *fanega*[7] of corn. This is understood to be for each house and not for each Indian, even though many Indian families live in such houses. It often happens that the pueblos increase or decrease in houses, or, if one tumbles down, its dwellers move to that of their relatives, and none of these pay tribute, except for the house in which they live. This works against the increase in houses, as tribute is collected as soon as the owners occupy them.

The *encomenderos* compel the Indians whose houses may have fallen down, or which they may have lost for other reasons, to pay tribute, even though they live in someone else's house. It is requested of your Majesty that the Indians of New Mexico do not pay tribute by the person, but by the house, as has always been done; that, as the *encomendero* is ready to receive the tribute of houses added to their pueblos, he should also be ready to lose and cease taking tribute from abandoned houses, even though the owners live in someone else's house.

It is requested that the Indians who, of their own will, move to live in other pueblos, being free, as they are, must not be hindered by their *encomenderos*, the governors, or other persons; that they may live freely in whatever pueblo they wish, and that, after they have established residence there for one year and a day, they become taxpayers at the place like the others of the same pueblo to the *encomendero* with whom they live. For the Indians suffer much harm when, if they do not get along with the *encomendero* in a pueblo where they do not find as good facilities for their work and farming as in some other one, they are forced to live there for the accommodation of the *encomendero*, whether they like it or not. If they have this freedom,

the *encomenderos* will help and accord good treatment to their tributary Indians so that they will not leave their pueblos and their tributes diminish.

It is requested that all the *caciques*[8], chief captains, governors, *alcaldes*[9], and *fiscales*[10] of the churches, on account of the big tasks they perform for the republic and the service of your Majesty, be exempt from tribute and personal service while they hold these offices. They are so busy in their offices that even their planted fields are cared for by others, as they are unable to do it themselves. The native lords and chieftains resent very much that they are compelled to pay tribute. Likewise, all the Indians who are choir singers and assistants in the churches are free only from personal service, but not from tribute, because of their regular attendance in church and in the schools.

It is requested that the Spanish governors be forbidden to issue warrants or permits to take Indian boys or girls from the pueblos on the pretext that they are orphans, and take them to serve permanently in the houses of the Spaniards where they remain as slaves. As a matter of fact, the orphans are well cared for at the homes of their grandparents or other relatives where they are brought up as if they were their own children. In case there should be any one without a home, the governor should not issue warrants without the consent of the ecclesiastical minister, who lives alone with the Indians and knows their needs and relieves them as much as he is able. This must be done so that the destitute Indian orphans may live freely with their relatives. The governors often take from the Spaniards some Indians who are serving the Spaniards well, in order to keep them for themselves. They take them without compensation, or, in payment, give them a permit to go to the pueblos to look for other boys and girls and to take them by force.

It is requested that the Indians taken in wars, whatever their nation, may not be given as slaves or sentenced to personal service outside of New Mexico, as is prescribed by royal decrees. On the contrary, they

---

7. Approximately 2 cubic feet, or just over a bushel and a half.
8. What Taíno peoples in the Caribbean called their chiefs, a term that the Spanish subsequently used to refer to Indian chiefs in North America, Mexico, Central America, and parts of South America.
9. Indian magistrates who often oversaw the apprehension of criminals, among other duties.
10. *Fiscales* acted as assistants to priests, helping with the management of parishes and the discipline of those who violated church teachings.

should be placed in convents of the friars or in houses of Spaniards or Indians of exemplary conduct so that they may be taught our holy Catholic faith with all kindness in order that they may become Christians. If any of them should run away they will tell the people of their nations of the good treatment accorded them and they will become inclined to our life and religion. This assignment to a convent may not be in the nature of a sale, transfer, or any other material consideration or period of time, but simply as an act of charity to instruct and convert them, which is the only purpose for which we have gone there. They must always be free in their lands, as they are often taken in wars and on other occasions, placed with an individual for many years who then transfers them to another individual for a consideration for the remainder of the time the assignment is to last. This is often done by the governors through a third party, and under this pretext they take many Indians, both men and women, to Mexico and other places to be sold.

It is requested that the Spanish governors be forbidden from depriving any native Indian chief of his post or authority, because of the fact that the Indians greatly resent seeing their leaders and chieftains mistreated.

QUESTIONS

1. For what reasons does Benavides request restrictions on the amount of tribute and personal service that governors could demand of Indians? For what reasons does he request greater regulation of the Indian slave trade to and through New Mexico?
2. What kind of relationship among friars, governors, and Indians does Benavides seek?
3. What can you learn about Pueblo life and politics from Benavides's petition?

2.4. JACQUES GRAVIER'S ACCOUNT OF THE MARRIAGE OF MARIE ROUENSA (1694)

Jacques Gravier was a Jesuit missionary sent to the Illinois country in 1687. His most important convert was Marie Rouensa. She was the daughter of the chief of the Kaskaskias, who comprised one branch of the Illinois Nation. When Rouensa was 17, her father pressured her to marry the French trader Michel Accault. Rouensa initially rejected the idea, and the passage below describes the conflict that followed. Gravier's account is part of *The Jesuit Relations*, a massive collection of documents generated by missionaries in New France.

Many struggles were needed before she [Marie Rouensa] could be induced to consent to the marriage, for she had resolved never to marry, in order that she might belong wholly to Jesus Christ. She answered her father and mother, when they brought her to me in company with the Frenchman whom they wished to have for a son-in-law,[11] that she did not wish to marry; that she had already given all her heart to God, and did not wish to share it. . . . her father, her mother, and still more the Frenchman who wished to marry her, were convinced that it was I who made her speak thus. . . .

Source: Reuben Gold Thwaites, ed., *The Jesuit Relations and Allied Documents: Travels and Explorations of the Jesuit Missionaries in New France, 1610–1791* (Cleveland: Burrows Brothers, 1896–1901), LXIV, 193–217.

11. Michel Accault.

That very night her father gathered the chiefs of the four villages together, and told them that, since I prevented the French from forming alliances with them,—and adding a number of other falsehoods to what he said,—he earnestly begged them to stop the women and children from coming to the chapel. He experienced no difficulty in making people who are themselves still but little inclined to Christianity believe all he wished. The prohibitions and threats did not prevent there being 50 persons present on the following day from the village of the *Peouareoua*,[12] with some *Kaskaskia*—as well as the girl, who exposed herself to ill treatment. . . .

[Finally, after much conflict, Marie Rouensa consented to the marriage after her father and mother agreed to be baptized.]

After the chief of the *Kaskaskia* had obtained his daughter's consent to the marriage with the Frenchman of whom I have spoken above, he informed all the chiefs of the villages, by considerable presents, that he was about to be allied to a Frenchman. The better to prepare herself for it, the girl made her first communion on the feast of the Assumption of Our Lady; she had prepared herself for it during more than 3 months—with such fervor, that she seemed fully penetrated by that great mystery. We may believe that Jesus Christ enriched her with many graces on the occasion of his first visit, and I observed in this girl the manifest effects of a good communion. As she had not forgotten what I had said of St. Henry on the day of his feast, and of St. Cunegonde, his wife, she hoped to persuade him whom she was about to marry to do the same.[13] The number of prayers she said to God with that object is incredible. I left her in that hope, for I had moreover fully instructed her regarding the obligations of marriage, and everything to which she pledged herself. Her husband has told me that she spoke to him in so tender and persuasive a manner that he could not avoid being touched by it, and that he was quite ashamed of being less virtuous than she. She has taken for her special patronesses the Christian Ladies who have sanctified themselves in the state of matrimony,—namely, St. Paula, St. Frances, St. Margaret, St. Elizabeth, and St. Bridget, whom she invokes many times during the day saying things to them that one would not believe from a young savage. The first conquest she made for God was to win her husband, who was famous in this *Ilinois* country for all his debaucheries. He is now quite changed, and he has admitted to me that he no longer recognizes himself, and can attribute his conversion solely to his wife's prayers and exhortations, and to the example that she gives him.

This good girl displays admirable care in getting the children and young girls of her village baptized, and it gives her great pleasure to be chosen as Godmother. She herself brings the children of her relatives, as soon as they are born—in order, as she says, that they may at once cease to be slaves of the Devil, and become children of God. And when she learns that a child who has been baptized is dead, she rejoices at this, and begs it to intercede with God for her, and for the whole village. The grown girls and the young women who have been baptized she induces, whenever she can, to come to her home, that she may instruct them; and she tries to inspire them with horror for dances, for night assemblies, and for evil of all kinds, and to instruct them regarding confession. . . . Her discretion and virtue give her marvelous authority, especially over those to whom she speaks of prayer without even any aged women finding fault with her—reproving them sometimes more energetically than I myself would do. What efforts did she not make to induce her father and mother to become Christians! She frequently added tears to her entreaties; and, since their baptism, she ceases not to remind them of the promises that they made to God.

QUESTIONS

1. Why did the arrival of missionaries spur conflict within Indian communities?
2. Why did Marie Rouensa's father pressure her to marry a Frenchman?
3. Marie Rouensa was one of many Indian women who found Catholicism appealing during a time of great change. How did Rouensa's Catholic faith empower her?

---

12. The Peoria Indians, a branch of the Illinois Nation.
13. Cunigunde wanted to become a nun, but agreed to marry the Holy Roman Emperor Henry II and became his closest advisor. She remained devout and influenced her husband's religious beliefs; both became saints.

CHAPTER 3

FORGING TIGHTER BONDS, 1640 TO 1700

3.1. VISUAL DOCUMENT: RICHARD FORD, *A NEW MAP OF THE ISLAND OF BARBADOES* (1674)

In 1674, Richard Ford made the map below of the island of Barbados. Published in England, it was the first economic map of an English American colony ever printed and soon became part of an atlas of maps that England's Office of Trade and Plantations compiled in the 1680s. Ford's map features the name of each plantation, usually named after its owner, as well as the sugar mills that produced the island's main export.

Source: Courtesy of the John Carter Brown Library at Brown University.

QUESTIONS

1. What can you learn about Barbados in the 1670s from Ford's map?

2. What impression of Barbados did Ford seek to give English users of his map?

3. What features of life and society in Barbados did Ford choose to ignore or leave out?

3.2. COMMITTEE OF THE MASSACHUSETTS BAY GENERAL COURT, "A MEMORANDUM OF INDIAN CHILDREN PUT FORTH INTO SERVICE TO THE ENGLISH" (1676)

In the wake of King Philip's War, New England colonists forced many Indian captives to become bound laborers. Those deemed too dangerous to remain in New England—mostly men, but also some boys (likely including Metacom's son)—were enslaved and sold in Bermuda or the West Indies. Indian children, including many orphaned by their parents' death in conflict or by execution by colonial authorities, became indentured servants. Below is a memorandum prepared by a committee that Massachusetts Bay legislators charged to bind out Indian children to colonists. One committee member, Daniel Gookin Sr., openly sympathized with the plight of Christian Indians during and after the war.

Beeing of those indians that came in & submitted with John Sachem of Packachooge, with the names of the persons with whome they were placed & the names and age of the children & the names of their relations & the places they Did belong to, By Mr Daniel Gookin Senr, Thomas Prentis Capt' & Mr Edward Oakes, who were a comittee appointed by the Counsel to mannage y^{tl} affayr. The termes & conditions vpon wch they are to serve is to be ordered by the Gen[eral] Court who are to provide y^t the children bee religiously educated & taught to read the English tounge

2 Boy A maid	To Samuel Simonds Esq. a boy named John his father named Alwitankus late of quantisit his father & mother p'ent[1] both consenting the boys age about 12 years	1 Boy	To Leift Jonathan Danforth of [Billericay?] a boy aged twelve yeares, son to papamech alius David late of Warwick or Cowesit.
	To him a girle named Hester her father & mother dead late of Nashaway her age ten years her onkel named John woosumpigin of Naticke	2 Boyes	To Mathew Bridge of CamBridge two Boyes the one named Jabez aged about ten yeares the other named Joseph aged six yeares their father named woompthe late of Packachooge F one or both these boyes is away with his father 8 ber[2] 17th
1 Boy	To Thomas Danforth esq a boy aged about 13 yeares his name John	1676	

Source: Proceedings of the Colonial Society of Massachusetts 19 (1918): 25–28.

1. An abbreviation for "present."
2. October

3 A boy & two Girls	To Mr Jerimiah Shepard of Rowley a boy named Absolom his father of the same name late of Manehage aged about ten yeares. To him a girle sister to the Lad named Sarah aged eleven yeares. These [illegible] of Naticke. To him another girle aged about 8 yeares her named Jane her father & mother dead.
1 Mayd	To Mrs Mitchell of Cambridg widdow a maid named Margaret aged about twelve yeares, her father named Suhunnick of quantisit her mother dead.
1 Boy	To Thomas Jacob of Ipswich a boy aged ten yeares, on wennaputanan his guardian & on upacunt of quantisitt his grand mother was present. The Boy [illegible].
1 Boy	To on Goodman Read a Tanner of cambridge a Boy named John aged about thirteen yeares his father Dead.
1 Boy	To Mr Jacob Green of Charel Towne a boy aged about seaven yeares his parrents Dead Late of quantisit but his mother of Narraganset.
1 Boy	To Thomas Woolson of Wattertowne a boy aged about 14 yeares his name John his father dead who was of Cowesit or warwick, his mother p'sent.
1 Boy	To Ciprian Steuens of Rumny Marsh but late of Lancaster a boy aged about six yeares son to nohanet of Chobnakonkonon. The Boy named Samuel.
1 Mayd	To Thomas Eliot of Boston a carpenter a maid aged about ten yeares her name Rebecka.
1 Boy	To Jacob Green Junior of Charles towne a Boy named Peter aged nine years his father dead his mother p'sent named nannantum of quantisit.
1 Boy	To on Goodman Greenland a carpenter of Charles towne on misticke side a boy named Tom aged twelve yeares his father named santeshe of Pakachooge.
1 Girle	To Mr Edmund Batter of Salem a maid named Abigal aged sixteen her mother a widow named quanshishe late of Shookannet Beyond mendon.
2 a Boy A girle	To Daniel Gookin Senr A Boy named Joshua aged about eight yeares son to William wunuko late of magunkoog; his father dead. To him a girle aged about six yeares daughter to the widow quinshiske late of Shookanet beyond mendon
1 Girle	To Andrew Bordman Tayler of cambridge a girle named Anne sister to ye Last named.
1 Boy	To Thomas Prentis Junior son to Capt Prentis of Cambridge village a boy named John son to William Wunnako late of magnkoy that was executed for Thomas Burney, aged thirteen.
1 Boy	To Benjamin Mills of Dedham a boy aged about six years is [named?] Joseph Spoonans late of Marlboro.
1 Boy	To Mr Edward Jackson a Boy named Joseph aged about 12 yeares Late of magalygook cosen[3] to Pyambow of Naticke.
1 Mayd	To Widdow Jackson of Cambridge village a girle named Hope aged nine yeare her parents dead who wer of Narraganset.
1 Boy	To old Goodman Myles of Dedham a boy of [ ] yeares old. son to Annaweeken Decesed who was late of Hassanamesit his mother p'sent.
1 Boy	To Capt. Thomas Prentis a Boy named Joseph son to Annaweken deceased Brother to the last named aged about 11 yeares F this boy was after taken from Capt Prentice & sent up Mr Stoughton for [ ] Capt Prentis is to bee considered about it for hee has taken more care & paynes about those indians.
1 Boy	To John Smith of Dedham a boy aged about eight yeares his father dead late of Marlborow hee is Brother to James Printers wife
1 Mayd	To Mr John Flint [?] of Concord a mayd aged about [ ] yeares [illegible]
1 Boy	To Mr Jonathan Wade of mistick a Boy named Tom Aged about 11 yeares sonne to William Wunakhow of Magunkgog deceased
1 Mayd	To Mr Nathaniel Wade of mistick a maid aged about ten years daughter to Jame Natomet [?] late of Packachooge her father & mother dead

---

3. Cousin.

It is humbly proposed to the Honble Generall Court, to set the time these children shall serve; & if not less y^{n4} till they come to 20 yeares of age. unto wch those y^t had relations seemed willing. and also that the Court lay som penalty upon them if they runne away before the time expire & on their parents or kindred y^t shall entice or harborr & conceale y^{m5} if they should runne away.

> *Signed By the Comitee*
> *Above named   Daniel Gookin Senr*
> *Edward Oakes.*
> *Cambridge*
> *8 ber 28 1676*

---

4. Than.
5. Them.

QUESTIONS

1. Under what terms were the Indian children bound out to serve the colonists?

2. What can you learn about the lives of Indian children from this memorandum? What does it tell you about the circumstances that brought them to be bound out and the lives that they might have lived once they became servants?

3. In the wake of King Philip's War, why did the Massachusetts legislators target Indian children to a greater degree than adults for servitude?

3.3. DECLARATION OF JOSEPHE FOLLOWING THE PUEBLO REVOLT (1681)

According to Spanish accounts of the time, the coordinated attacks that drove Spanish colonists from New Mexico in 1680 took the Spanish by surprise. As they regrouped after having fled for their lives, Spanish leaders, including the colony's governor Antonio de Otermín, sought to collect as much information as they could about what had happened. A key part of that process was the interrogation of Pueblo prisoners. Below is an excerpt from the interrogation of one such prisoner, conducted in late 1681.

... [O]n the 19th day of the month of December, 1681, . . ., his lordship caused to appear before him an Indian prisoner named Josephe, able to speak the Castilian language,[6] a servant of Sargento Mayor Sebastián de Herrera who fled from him and went among the apostates. . . .

Asked what causes or motives the said Indian rebels had for renouncing the law of God and obedience to his Majesty, and for committing so many kinds of crimes, and who were the instigators of the rebellion, and what he had heard while he was among the apostates, he said that the prime movers of the rebellion were two Indians of San Juan, one named El Popé and the other El Taqu, and another from Taos named Saca, and another from San Ildefonso named Francisco. He knows that these were the principals, and the causes

---

Source: Revolt of the Pueblo Indians of New Mexico and Otermín's Attempted Reconquest 1680–1682, ed. Charles Wilson Hackett (Albuquerque: University of New Mexico Press, 1942), 9:238–42.

6. Castilian is what we now call Spanish.

they gave were alleged ill treatment and injuries received from the present secretary, Francisco Xavier, and the maestre de campo, Alonso García, and from the sargentos mayores, Luis de Quintana and Diego López, because they beat them, took away what they had, and made them work without pay. Thus he replies.

Asked if he has learned or it has come to his notice during the time that he has been here the reason why the apostates burned the images, churches, and things pertaining to divine worship, making a mockery and a trophy of them, killing the priests and doing the other things they did, he said that he knows and has heard it generally stated that while they were besieging the villa the rebellious traitors burned the church and shouted in loud voices, "Now the God of the Spaniards, who was their father, is dead, and Santa María, who was their mother, and the saints, who were pieces of rotten wood," saying that only their own god lived. Thus they ordered all the temples and images, crosses and rosaries burned, and this function being over, they all went to bathe in the rivers, saying that they thereby washed away the water of baptism. For their churches, they placed on the four sides and in the center of the plaza some small circular enclosures of stone where they went to offer flour, feathers, and the seed of maguey,[7] maize, and tobacco, and performed other superstitious rites, giving the children to understand that they must all do this in the future. The captains and chiefs ordered that the names of Jesus and of Mary should nowhere be uttered, and that they should discard their baptismal names, and abandon the wives whom God had given them in matrimony, and take the ones that they pleased. He saw that as soon as the remaining Spaniards had left, they ordered all the estufas[8] erected, which are their houses of idolatry, and danced throughout the kingdom the dance of the cazina,[9] making many masks for it in the image of the devil. . . .

. . . He said that what he has stated in his declaration is the truth and what he knows, under charge of his oath, which he affirms and ratifies, this, his said declaration, being read to him. He did not sign because of not knowing how, nor does he know his age. Apparently he is about twenty years old.

QUESTIONS

1. What, according to Josephe, caused the Pueblo Revolt?
2. The Pueblo Revolt is an example of a nativist movement in which Indigenous peoples seek to rid themselves of foreign influences. Which Spanish influences did the Pueblos target?
3. Context is important in evaluating documents. A Spanish official wrote this document after capturing and interrogating Josephe, who was likely coerced into testifying. How might Josephe's interrogator or his status as a prisoner of war have shaped this document?

---

7. agave
8. By "estufas," the Spanish writer meant kivas, subterranean structures in which Pueblos held religious ceremonies.
9. Kachinas, the ancestral and otherworldly beings whom Pueblos believed brought rain and harmony.

3.4. GERMANTOWN QUAKER MEETING, "REASONS WHY WE ARE AGAINST THE TRAFFIC OF MEN-BODY" (1688)

As Pennsylvania's population and economy grew rapidly during the 1680s, so did the nascent colony's population of enslaved Africans and African Americans, a development that alarmed some. In 1688, four German colonists who belonged to the Germantown Quaker Meeting penned the petition below and requested that the monthly meeting consider it. Included as well are that meeting's response and the responses of the quarterly meeting in Philadelphia and the monthly meeting in Burlington, New Jersey. As Chapter 5 discusses, Pennsylvania Quakers did spearhead an antislavery initiative in the Anglo-Atlantic world, but not until the 1760s.

This is to the monthly meeting held at Richard Worrell's:

These are the reasons why we are against the traffic of men-body, as followeth: Is there any that would be done or handled at this manner? viz., to be sold or made a slave for all the time of his life? How fearful and faint-hearted are many at sea, when they see a strange vessel, being afraid it should be a Turk, and they should be taken, and sold for slaves into Turkey. Now, what is *this* better done, than Turks do? Yea, rather it is worse for them, which say they are Christians; for we hear that the most part of such negers are brought hither against their will and consent, and that many of them are stolen. Now, though they are black, we cannot conceive there is more liberty to have them slaves, as [than] it is to have other white ones. There is a saying, that we should do to all men like as we will be done ourselves; making no difference of what generation, descent, or colour they are. And those who steal or rob men, and those who buy or purchase them, are they not all alike? Here is liberty of conscience, which is right and reasonable; here ought to be likewise liberty of the body, except of evil-doers, which is another case. But to bring men hither, or to rob and sell them against their will, we stand against. In Europe, there are many oppressed for conscience-sake; and here there are those oppressed which are of a black colour. And we who know that men must not commit adultery—some do commit adultery *in* others, separating wives from their husbands, and giving them to others: and some sell the children of these poor creatures to other men. Ah! do consider well this thing, you who do it, if you would be done at this manner—and if it is done according to Christianity! You surpass Holland and Germany in this thing. This makes an ill report in all those countries of Europe, where they hear of [it,] that the Quakers do here handel men as they handel there the cattle. And for that reason some have no mind or inclination to come hither. And who shall maintain this your cause, or plead for it? Truly, we cannot do so, except you shall inform us better hereof, viz.: that Christians have liberty to practise these things. Pray, what thing in the world can be done worse towards us, than if men should rob or steal us away, and sell us for slaves to strange countries; separating husbands from their wives and children. Being now this is not done in the manner we would be done at, [by]; therefore, we contradict, and are against this traffic of men-body. And we who profess that it is not lawful to steal, must, likewise, avoid to purchase such things as are stolen,

Source: George H. Moore, *Notes on the History of Slavery in Massachusetts* (New York, 1866), 74–78.

but rather help to stop this robbing and stealing, if possible. And such men ought to be delivered out of the hands of the robbers, and set free as in Europe. Then is Pennsylvania to have a good report, instead, it hath now a bad one, for this sake, in other countries: Especially whereas the Europeans are desirous to know in what manner *the Quakers* do rule in *their* province; and most of them do look upon us with an envious eye. But if this is done well, what shall we say is done evil?

If once these slaves (which they say are so wicked and stubborn men,) should join themselves—fight for their freedom, and handel their masters and mistresses, as they did handel them before; will these masters and mistresses take the sword at hand and war against these poor slaves, like, as we are able to believe, some will not refuse to do? Or, have these poor negroes not as much right to fight for their freedom, as you have to keep them slaves?

Now consider well this thing, if it is good or bad. And in case you find it to be good to handel these blacks in that manner, we desire and require you hereby lovingly, that you may inform us herein, which at this time never was done, viz., that Christians have such a liberty to do so. To the end we shall be satisfied on this point, and satisfy likewise our good friends and acquaintances in our native country, to whom it is a terror, or fearful thing, that men should be handelled so in Pennsylvania.

This is from our meeting at Germantown, held ye 18th of the 2d month, 1688, to be delivered to the monthly meeting at Richard Worrell's.

Garret Henderich,
Derick op de Graeff,
Francis Daniel Pastorius,
Abram op de Graeff.

At our monthly meeting, at Dublin, ye 30th 2d mo., 1688, we having inspected ye matter, above mentioned, and considered of it, we find it so weighty that we think it not expedient for us to meddle with it *here*, but do rather commit it to ye consideration of ye quarterly meeting; ye tenor of it being related to ye truth.

On behalf of ye monthly meeting, Jo. Hart.

This above mentioned, was read in our quarterly meeting, at Philadelphia, the 4th of ye 4th mo., '88, and was from thence recommended to the yearly meeting, and the above said Derrick, and the other two mentioned therein, to present the same to ye above said meeting, it being a thing of too great weight for this meeting to determine.

Signed by order of ye meeting. Anthony Morris.

The minutes of the Yearly Meeting, held at Burlington in the same year, record the result of this first effort among the Quakers.

At a Yearly Meeting, held at Burlington the 5th day of the 7th Month, 1688.

A paper being here presented by some German Friends Concerning the Lawfulness & Unlawfulness of Buying & Keeping of Negroes It was adjudged not to be so proper for this Meeting to give a Positive Judgment in the Case It having so general a Relation to many other Parts & therefore at present they Forbear It.

QUESTIONS

1. On what grounds do Pastorius and his peers oppose slavery and the Atlantic slave trade? Keep in mind as you answer that these were Quaker men writing to other Quakers in 1688.
2. What became of the Germantown petition? In what manner did superior meetings respond to it?
3. In their petition, the authors mention several other nations, including both Christian and Islamic powers. Why do you think they frame their plea in a global context?

CHAPTER 4

ACCELERATING THE PACE OF CHANGE, c. 1690 TO 1730

4.1. *BOSTON NEWS-LETTER*, EDITORIAL FAVORING INDENTURED SERVITUDE OVER SLAVERY (1706)

Although relatively few enslaved Africans and African Americans lived in Massachusetts in the early 18th century, the black population there was growing, largely because of Massachusetts merchants' engagement in the Atlantic slave trade. In 1706, an anonymous author composed and published an editorial on slavery in the *Boston News-Letter*, North America's first established newspaper. It was perhaps the first editorial to appear in a North American newspaper, and it is reprinted below in its entirety.

By last Years Bill of Mortality for the Town of Boston in Numb 100 *News Letter*,[1] we are furnished with a List of 44 Negroes dead last year, which being computed one with another at 30 *l.* per Head, amounts to the Sum of One Thousand three hundred and Twenty Pounds, of which we would make this Remark: That the Importing of Negroes into this or the Neighbouring Provinces is not so beneficial either to the Crown or Country, as White Servants would be.

For Negroes do not carry Arms to defend the Country as Whites do:

Negroes are generaly Eye-Servants[2], great Thieves, much addicted to stealing, Lying, and Purloining.

They do not People our Country as Whites would do whereby we should be strengthened against an Enemy.

By Encouraging the importing of White Men Servants, allowing somewhat to the importer, most Husbandmen in the Country might be furnished with Servants for 8, 9, or 10 *l.* a Head, who are not able to Launch out 40 or 50 *l.* for a Negro the now common Price.

Source: Elizabeth Donnan, ed., *Documents Illustrative of the History of the Slave Trade to America*, vol. 3 (Washington, D.C.: Carnegie Institution of Washington, 1932), 21–23.

1. *Boston News Letter*, March 18, 1706.
2. A servant whom one must supervise constantly.

A Man then might buy a White Man Servant we suppose for 10 *l.* to Serve 4 years, and Boys for the same price to Serve 6, 8 or 10 years: If a White Servant die, the Loss exceeds not 10 *l.* but if a Negro dies 'tis a very great Loss to the Husbandman. Three years Interest of the price of the Negro, will near upon if not altogether purchase a White Man Servant.

If Necessity call for it, that the Husbandman must fit out a man against the Enemy; if he has a Negro he cannot send him, but if he has a White Servant, 'twill answer the end, and perhaps save his Son at home.

Were Merchants and Masters Encouraged as already said to bring in Men Servants, there needed not be such complaint against Superiors Impressing our Children to the War, there would then be Men enough to be had without Impressing.

The bringing in of such servants would much enrich this Province, because Husbandmen would not only be able far better to manure what Lands are already under Improvement, but would also improve a great deal more that now lyes waste under Woods, and enable this Province to set about raising of Naval Stores, which would be greatly advantagious to the Crown of England, and this Province. . . .

Suppose the Government here should allow Forty Shillings per head for five years, to such as should Import every of those years 100 White Men Servants, and each to serve 4 Years, the cost would be but 200 *l.* a year, and a 1000 for the five years: the first 100 servants being free the 4th year, they serve the 5th for Wages, and the 6th there is 100 that goes out into the Woods, and settles a 100 Families to strengthen and Baracade us from the Indians, and so a 100 Families more every year successively.

And here you see that in one year the Town of Boston has lost 1320 *l.* by 44 Negroes, which is also a Loss to this Country in general, and for a less Loss, (if it may improperly be so called) for a 1000 *l.* the Country may have 500 Men in 5 years time for the 44 Negroes dead in one year.

A certain person within these 6 years had two Negroes dead computed both at 60 *l.* which would have procured him six white Servants at 10 *l.* per head to have Served 24 years, at 4 years a piece, without running such a great risque, and the Whites would have strengthened the Country, that Negroes do not. 'Twould do wel[l] that none of those Servants be liable to be Impressed during their Service of Agreement at their first Landing.

That such Servants being Sold or Transported out of this Province during the time of their Service, the person that buys them be liable to pay 3 *l.* into the Treasury.

QUESTIONS

1. On what grounds does the author favor indentured servitude over slavery?
2. In what ways did then-current events probably influence the content and tone of the editorial?
3. What elements of racial thinking are present in the essay?

4.2. VISUAL DOCUMENT: GUILLAUME DE L'ISLE, CARTE DE LA LOUISIANE ET DU COURS DU MISSISSIPI (MAP OF LOUISIANA AND COURSE OF THE MISSISSIPPI) (1718)

Guillaume de L'Isle was one of the most talented cartographers of his day. Born in Paris in 1675, de L'Isle studied at the Académie Royale des Sciences. He was among the first cartographers to benefit from the scientific revolution, incorporating more exact measurements and visual enhancements using perspective. Although he never traveled to the Americas, de L'Isle received many reports from French explorers and officials in the colonies. De'Isle is probably most famous for the map below, created for the court of King Louis XV. The most detailed map of North America up to that point, the "Carte de la Louisiane," was subsequently copied by many cartographers.

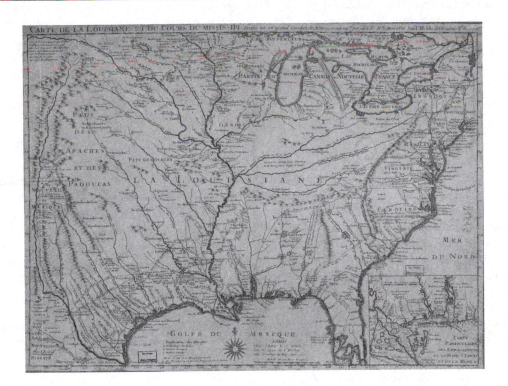

Source: Library of Congress Geography and Maps Division, Washington, D.C.

QUESTIONS

1. Maps do not necessarily reflect reality; they are often biased and may be aspirational. (Remember that, in 1718, less than 400 French colonists lived in Louisiana.) In what ways is Guillaume de L'Isle's map biased or aspirational?

2. How are Indian polities depicted on the map? What does this reveal about French colonialism in North America?

3. How do you think this map was received by the court of King Louis XV? Was it more of a political document or a scientific document?

4.3. A FRENCH COLONIST'S ACCOUNT OF THE ORIGINS OF THE FIRST FRANCO-CHICKASAW WAR (1736)

In the aftermath of the Natchez War (1729–1731), French Louisiana waged a series of wars against the Chickasaw Nation. The Chickasaws, whose trade alliance with the British ensured steady access to firearms, prevailed in every conflict. The account below comes from Antoine Simon Le Page du Pratz, a French planter who settled near the Natchez Indians. Le Page du Pratz was keenly interested in Native Americans, whom he learned about, in part, from one of his slaves, a Chitimacha Indian woman who became Le Page du Pratz's concubine. Below is an early English translation of Le Page du Pratz's *Histoire de la Louisiane* (first published in France in 1758) in which he recounts the origins of the 1736 Franco-Chickasaw War.

The War with the Chicasaws[3] was owing to their having received and adopted the Natchez: though in this respect they acted only according to an inviolable usage and sacred custom, established among all the nations of North America; that when a nation, weakened by war, retires for shelter to another, who are willing to adopt them, and is pursued thither by their enemies, this is in effect to declare war against the nation adopting.

But M. de Biainville,[4] whether displeased with this act of hospitality, or losing sight of this unalterable law, constantly prevailing among those nations,

sent word to the Chicasaws, to give up the Natchez. In answer to his demand they alledged, that the Natchez having demanded to be incorporated with them, were accordingly received and adopted; so as now to constitute but one nation, or people, under the name of Chicasaws, that of Natchez being entirely abolished. Besides, added they, had Biainville received our enemies, should we go to demand them? or, if we did, would they be given up?

Notwithstanding this answer, M. de Biainville made warlike preparations against the Chicasaws, sent off

Source: Antoine Simon Le Page du Pratz, *The History of Louisiana, or of the Western Parts of Virginia and Carolina* (London: T. Becket, 1774), 96–97.

3. The Chickasaws.
4. This refers to Monsieur de Bienville, whose full name was Jean-Baptiste Le Moyne, Sieur de Bienville. He then served as governor of Louisiana.

Captain le Blanc, with six armed boats under his command; one laden with gun-powder, the rest with goods, the whole allotted for the war against the Chicasaws; the Captain at the same time carrying orders to M. d'Artaguette, Commandant of the Post of the Illinois,[5] to prepare to set out at the head of all the troops, inhabitants and Indians, he could march from the Illinois, in order to be at the Chicasaws the 10th of May following, as the Governor himself was to be there at the same time.

The Chicasaws, apprized of the warlike preparations of the French, resolved to guard the Missisipi, imagining they would be attacked on that side. In vain they attempted to surprize M. le Blanc's convoy, which got safe to the Arkansas, where the gun-powder was left, for reasons no one can surmise.

From thence he had no cross [adjacent] to the Illinois, at which place he delivered the orders the Governor had dispatched for M. d'Artaguette; who finding a boat laden with gun-powder, designed for his post, and for the service of the war intended against the Chicasaws, left at the Arkansas, sent off the same day a boat to fetch it up; which on its return was taken by a party of Chicasaws; who killed all but M. du Tissenet, junior, and one Rosalie, whom they made slaves.

QUESTIONS

1. According to Le Page du Pratz, what was the main cause of the 1736 Franco-Chickasaw War?
2. How did Chickasaw understandings of nationality differ from those of the French?
3. In the 18th century, Native American nations faced many threats from colonial powers, but some nations developed strategies for maintaining or enhancing their power. What strategies did the Chickasaws use?

4.4. EXCERPTS FROM SAUKAMAPPEE'S ACCOUNT OF THE ADVENT OF HORSES AND GUNS TO THE BLACKFEET, AS TOLD TO DAVID THOMPSON (1787–1788)

Fur trader David Thompson spent part of the winter of 1787–1788 living among the Piegans, who belonged to the Blackfoot Confederacy and lived in what is today Montana. While there, he met Saukamappee, a Cree whom the Piegans had adopted. Saukamappee, then probably in his late seventies, told Thompson about his youth and Piegan history. Here Saukamappee recalls a battle that took place around 1730 between the Piegans and their allies, who were armed with guns and metal weapons, and their longtime foes, the Shoshones (whom Saukamappee and his people called "Snakes"), who fought on horseback. He also recounts what the Piegans did after their victory.

By this time the affairs of both parties had much changed; we had more guns and iron headed arrows than before; but our enemies the Snake Indians and their allies had Misstutim (Big Dogs, that is, Horses) on which they rode, swift as the Deer, on which they dashed at the Peeagans, and with their

Source: Richard Glover, ed., *David Thompson's Narrative, 1784–1812* (Toronto: Champlain Society, 1962), 241–43.

5. French Louisiana then claimed land extending to modern-day Illinois, named after the Illinois Nation which, at that time, dominated the region.

stone Pukamoggan knocked them on the head, and they had thus lost several of their best men. This news we did not well comprehend and it alarmed us, for we had no idea of Horses and could not make out what they were. Only three of us went and I should not have gone, had not my wife's relations frequently intimated, that her father's medicine bag would be honored by the scalp of a Snake Indian. When we came to our allies, the great War Tent [was made] with speeches, feasting and dances as before; and when the War Chief had viewed us all it was found between us and the Stone Indians we had ten guns and each of us about thirty balls, and powder for the war, and we were considered the strength of the battle. After a few days march our scouts brought us word that the enemy was near in a large war party, but had no Horses with them, for at that time they had very few of them. When we came to meet each other, as usual, each displayed their numbers, weapons and shiel[d]s, in all which they were superior to us, except our guns which were not shown, but kept in their leathern cases, and if we had shown [them], they would have taken them for long clubs. For a long time they held us in suspense; a tall Chief was forming a strong party to make an attack on our centre, and the others to enter into combat with those opposite to them; We prepared for the battle the best we could. Those of us who had guns stood in the front line, and each of us [had] two balls in his mouth, and a load of powder in his left hand to reload.

We noticed they had a great many short stone clubs for close combat, which is a dangerous weapon, and had they made a bold attack on us, we must have been defeated as they were more numerous and better armed than we were, for we could have fired our guns no more than twice; and were at a loss what to do on the wide plain, and each Chief encouraged his men to stand firm. Our eyes were all on the tall Chief and his motions, which appeared to be contrary to the advice of several old Chiefs, all this time we were about the strong flight of an arrow from each other. At length the tall chief retired and they formed their long usual line by placing their shields on the ground to touch each other, the shield having a breadth of full three feet or more. We sat down opposite to them and most of us waited for the night to make a hasty retreat. The War Chief was close to us, anxious to see the effect

of our guns. The lines were too far asunder for us to make a sure shot, and we requested him to close the line to about sixty yards, which was gradually done, and lying flat on the ground behind the shields, we watched our opportunity when they drew their bows to shoot at us, their bodies were then exposed and each of us, as opportunity offered, fired with deadly aim, and either killed, or severely wounded, every one we aimed at.

The War Chief was highly pleased, and the Snake Indians finding so many killed and wounded kept themselves behind their shields; the War Chief then desired we would spread ourselves by two's throughout the line, which we did, and our shots caused consternation and dismay along their whole line. The battle had begun about Noon, and the Sun was not yet half down, when we perceived some of them had crawled away from their shields, and were taking to flight. The War Chief seeing this went along the line and spoke to every Chief to keep his Men ready for a charge of the whole line of the enemy, of which he would give the signal; this was done by himself stepping in front with his Spear, and calling on them to follow him as he rushed on their line, and in an instant the whole of us followed him, the greater part of the enemy took to flight, but some fought bravely and we lost more than ten killed and many wounded; Part of us pursued, and killed a few, but the chase had soon to be given over, for at the body of every Snake Indian killed, there were five or six of us trying to get his scalp, or part of his clothing, his weapons, or something as a trophy of the battle. As there were only three of us, and seven of our friends, the Stone Indians, we did not interfere, and got nothing.

The next morning the War Chief made a speech, praising their bravery, and telling them to make a large War Tent to commemorate their victory, to which they directly set to work and by noon it was finished.

The War Chief now called on all the other Chiefs to assemble their men and come to the Tent. In a short time they came, all those who had lost relations had their faces blackened; those who killed an enemy, or wished to be thought so, had their faces blackened with red streaks on the face, and those who had no pretensions to the one, or the other, had their faces red with ochre. We did not paint our faces until the War

Chief told us to paint our foreheads and eyes black, and the rest of the face of dark red ochre, as having carried guns, and to distinguish us from all the rest. Those who had scalps now came forward with the scalps neatly stretched on a round willow with a handle to the frame; they appeared to be more than fifty, and excited loud shouts and the war whoop of victory. When this was over the War Chief told them that if any one had a right to the scalp of an enemy as a war trophy it ought to be us, who with our guns had gained the victory, when from the numbers of our enemies we were anxious to leave the field of battle; and that ten scalps must be given to us; this was soon collected, and he gave to each of us a Scalp.

QUESTIONS

1. How, according to Saukamappee, did the Piegans initially react to Shoshone use of horses, and how did the Shoshones initially react to Piegan use of firearms?

2. How did firearms change battle strategy and outcomes?

3. How did firearms influence the ways that Piegans regarded Saukamappee?

CHAPTER 5

BATTLING FOR SOULS, MINDS, AND THE HEART OF NORTH AMERICA, 1730 TO 1763

5.1. ENGLISH COPY OF A CATAWBA DEERSKIN MAP (c. 1721)

Around 1721, Catawba leaders presented this map to Francis Nicholson, the newly appointed governor of South Carolina. Previously, Nicholson had served as governor of Virginia, and throughout his political career he solicited and collected Indian maps. Mapmaking was common among Native Americans, but relatively few Indian maps from the colonial era survive. Those that remain fall into two broad categories. Some emphasize geographical knowledge, while others—like this Catawba map—stress social and political relationships. This map shows Virginia at the bottom right and the port of Charleston, South Carolina, at the left. The circles represent Native groups: Most are Catawba towns, but two of the circles—"Cherrikies" (Cherokees) and "Chickisa" (Chickasaw)—are nations.

Source: Library of Congress.

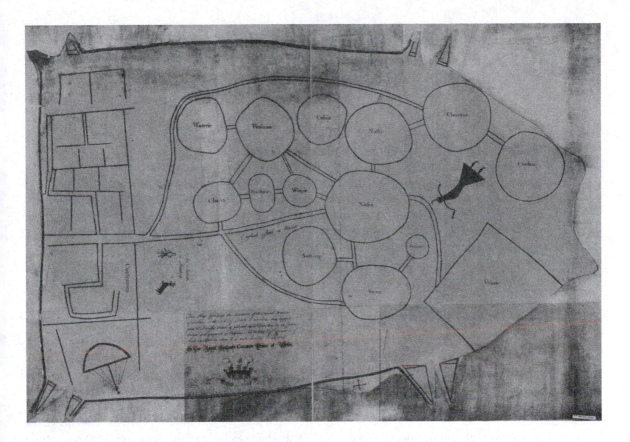

QUESTIONS

1. Reflect on the symbols used in the map. What do the connected lines represent? What does the absence of connected lines represent? Why did the mapmaker use circles for some peoples and squares for others?

2. Why are European colonies and towns included in this map?

3. Why do you think that Governor Francis Nicholson and other colonial leaders requested Indian maps?

5.2. FUTURE RESIDENTS OF GRACIA REAL DE MOSE, FLORIDA, LETTER TO PHILIP V, KING OF SPAIN (1738)

During the 18th and early 19th centuries, enslaved Africans and African Americans in South Carolina and Georgia sought freedom by fleeing south to Florida when it was under Spanish rule. Even though royal orders dating back to 1693 granted refuge and freedom to enslaved people who converted to Catholicism, Spanish colonists sometimes re-enslaved the fugitives. Francisco Menéndez, an African man who had escaped slavery in South Carolina, wrote petitions in Spanish imploring Philip V to intervene. In 1738, the royal governor recognized the freedom of all Carolina runaways, which prompted the letter of thanks to Philip V that appears below.

My lord,

All the Black people who escaped from the English plantations, obedient and loyal slaves to Your Majesty, declare that Your Majesty has done us true charity in ordering us to be given freedom for having come to this country and for being Christian and following the true religion that saves us.

Disobeying a very high and sacred law, they bound us and made us slaves for many years, putting us through many miseries and much hunger. But obeying laws which Your Majesty decreed, the present Governor, Don Manuel de Montiano, has set us free, for which we greatly appreciate Your Majesty and thank him for this most royal kindness.

Likewise, the Governor has offered and assured us that he will establish a place for us, which is called Gracia Real, where we may serve God and Your Majesty, cultivating the land so that there may be fruit in this country.

We promise Your Majesty that, whenever the opportunity arises, we will be the cruelest enemies to the English and will risk our lives in the service of Your Majesty, even to spilling the last drop of blood, in defense of the great crown of Spain and our holy faith.

Thus Your Majesty may order any amount of service from us because we are his faithful slaves all of our life and we will always pray Our Lord to guard Your Majesty's life and the life of all the Royal Family throughout the slow years that we poor people need.

Saint Augustine, Florida, 10 June 1738.

QUESTION

1. How do the authors characterize the English? Why do they draw a contrast between the English and Spanish in this letter?
2. What did the authors of this letter promise Philip V? Why did they make such a promise?
3. What role did religion play in imperial rivalries?

Source: *Interpreting a Continent: Voices from Colonial America*, eds. Kathleen DuVal and John DuVal (Lanham, Md.: Rowan & Littlefield, 2009), 179–80. Translated by John DuVal from Audiencia de Santo Domingo 844, fol. 607, reel 15, P. K. Yonge Library, University of Florida, Gainesville.

5.3. CANASSATEGO (ONONDAGA), EXCERPTS FROM HIS RESPONSE TO A DELAWARE COMPLAINT CONCERNING THE WALKING PURCHASE (1742)

In 1736, the Iroquois League and Pennsylvania officials agreed that the Iroquois League would speak on behalf of all Indians who lived between the Iroquois homeland (in today's Upstate New York) and Philadelphia. The following year, Delaware Indians ceded about 1,200 square miles of land to Pennsylvania under the terms of the "Walking Purchase." Delawares issued a stream of protests concerning the "Walking Purchase" over the next few years, arguing that Pennsylvania officials had violated their agreement by dispatching runners along cleared and marked paths to claim as much territory as possible. In 1742, Onondaga chief and Iroquois spokesman Canassatego appeared at a treaty conference in Philadelphia and issued the following response to the Delaware delegation.

At a Council held at the Proprietors, July 12th. present: The Honble GEORGE THOMAS, Esqᵣ, Lieutenant Governor.

James Logan,
Clement Plumsted,
Thomas Laurence,
Abraham Taylor,
Robert Strettel,

Esqrs.

Mr. Richard Peters.

Canassatego,
Skick Calamy,

and sundry Chiefs of the six Nations.

Sassonan and Delawares.
Nutimus and ffork Indians.

Pisquetoman,
Cornelius Spring,
Nicholas Scull,

Interpreters to the ffork Indians.

Canassatego said,

"Brethren, the Governor, and Council:

"The other Day you informed Us of the Misbehaviour of our Cousins the Delawares with respect to their continuing to Claim and refusing to remove from some Land on the River Delaware, notwithstanding their Ancestors had sold it by Deed under their Hands & Seals to the Proprietors for a valuable Consideration, upwards of fifty Years ago, and notwithstanding that they them[s]elves had about—Years ago, after a long and full Examination, ratified that Deed of their Ancestors, and given a fresh one under their Hands and Seals, and then you requested Us to remove them, enforcing your Request with a String of Wampum. Afterwards you laid on the Table by Conrad Weiser our own Letters, some of our Cousins' Letters, and the several Writings to prove the Charge against our Cousins, with a Draught of the Land in Dispute. We now tell You we have Perused all these several Papers. We see with our own Eyes that they have been a very unruly People, and are altogether in the wrong in their Dealings with You. We have concluded to remove them, and Oblige them to go over the River Delaware, and to quit all Claim to any Lands on this side for the future, since they have received Pay for them and it is gone

Source: Pennsylvania Colonial Records, vol. 4 (Harrisburg, PA: 1851), 578–80.

through their Guts long ago. To confirm to You that we will see your Request Executed, we lay down this String of Wampum in return for your's."

Then turning to the Delawares, holding a Belt of Wampum in his Hand, he spoke to them as followeth:

"Cousins:

"Let this Belt of Wampum serve to Chastize You; You ought to be taken by the Hair of the Head and shak'd severely till you recover your Senses and become Sober; you don't know what Ground you stand on, nor what you are doing. Our Brother Onas'[1] Case is very just and plain, and his Intentions to preserve ffriendship; on the other Hand your Cause is bad, your Heart far from being upright, and you are maliciously bent to break the Chain of ffriendship with our Brother Onas. We have seen with our Eyes a Deed signed by nine of your Ancestors above fifty Years ago for this very Land, and a Release Sign'd not many Years since by some of your selves and Chiefs now living to the Number of 15 or Upwards. But how came you to take upon you to Sell Land at all? We conquer'd You, we made Women of you, you know you are Women, and can no more sell Land than Women. Nor is it fit you should have the Power of Selling Lands since you would abuse it. This Land that you Claim is gone through Your Guts. You have been furnished with Cloaths and Meat and Drink by the Goods paid you for it, and now You want it again like Children as you are. But what makes you sell Land in the Dark? Did you ever tell Us that you had sold this Land? did we ever receive any Part, even the Value of a Pipe Shank, from you for it? You have told Us a Blind story that you sent a Messenger to Us to inform Us of the Sale but he never came amongst Us, nor we never heard any thing about it. This is acting in the Dark, and very different from the Conduct our six Nations observe in their Sales of Land. On such Occasions they give Publick Notice and invite all the Indians of their united Nations, and give them a share of the Present they receive for their Lands. This is the behaviour of the wise United Nations, but we find you are none of our Blood. You Act a dishonest part not only in this but in other Matters. Your Ears are ever Open to slanderous

Reports about our Brethren. You receive them with as much greediness as Lewd Wom[e]n receive the Embraces of Bad Men. And for all these reasons we charge You to remove instantly. We don't give you the liberty to think about it. You are Women; take the Advice of a Wise Man and remove imediately. You may return to the other side of Delaware where you came from, but we don't know whether, Considering how you have demean'd your selves, you will be permitted to live there, or whether you have not swallowed that Land down your Throats as well as the Land on this side. We, therefore, Assign you two Places to go—either to Wyomin or Shamokin. You may go to either of these Places, and then we shall have you more under our Eye, and shall see how You behave. Don't deliberate, but remove away and take this Belt of Wampum."

This being interpreted by Conrad Weiser into English, and by Cornelius Spring into the Delaware language, Canassatego taking a String of Wampum added further:

"After our just reproof and absolute Order to depart from the Land, you are now to take Notice of what we have further to say to you. This String of Wampum serves to forbid You, Your Children and Grand Children, to the latest Posterity, for ever medling in Land Affairs, neither you nor any who shall descend from You, are ever hereafter to presume to sell any Land, for which Purpose you are to Preserve this string in Memory of what your Uncles have this Day given You in Charge. We have some other Business to transact with our Brethren, and therefore depart the Council and consider what has been said to you."

QUESTIONS

1. Why did Canassatego begin or end each statement by presenting wampum to the party he was addressing?
2. What did Canassatego want the Delawares to do?
3. On what grounds did Canassatego support Pennsylvania's side in the Walking Purchase dispute and assert the Iroquois League's influence over the Delawares?

---

1   The Iroquois called William Penn "Onas" (which means "pen," a pun on his name) and also used the term to refer to subsequent leaders of Pennsylvania.

5.4. BENJAMIN FRANKLIN, EXCERPTS FROM "OBSERVATIONS ON THE INCREASE OF MANKIND" (1751)

In 1751, Benjamin Franklin penned the essay "Observations on the Increase of Mankind," excerpts of which appear below. The passage of the Iron Act of 1750, which sought to restrict the development of colonial British North America's iron industry, seems to have prompted him to write it. Most of the essay focuses on population growth in the colonies, which, Franklin argued, made North America increasingly important to the economic development and strategic needs of the British Empire. The essay was first published in London in 1755. Franklin's political enemies capitalized on some of its contents a decade later, as Chapter 5 of the text discusses.

6. Land being thus plenty in America, and so cheap as that a labouring Man, that understands Husbandry, can in a short Time save Money enough to purchase a Piece of new Land sufficient for a Plantation, whereon he may subsist a Family; such are not afraid to marry; for if they even look far enough forward to consider how their Children when grown up are to be provided for, they see that more Land is to be had at Rates equally easy, all Circumstances considered.

7. Hence Marriages in America are more general, and more generally early, than in Europe. And if it is reckoned there, that there is but one Marriage per Annum among 100 Persons, perhaps we may here reckon two; and if in Europe they have but 4 Births to a Marriage (many of their Marriages being late) we may here reckon 8, of which if one half grow up, and our Marriages are made, reckoning one with another at 20 Years of Age, our People must at least be doubled every 20 Years.

8. But notwithstanding this Increase, so vast is the Territory of North-America, that it will require many Ages to settle it fully; and till it is fully settled, Labour will never be cheap here, where no Man continues long a Labourer for others, but gets a Plantation of his own, no Man continues long a Journeyman to a Trade, but goes among those new Settlers, and sets up for himself, &c. Hence Labour is no cheaper now, in Pennsylvania, than it was 30 Years ago, tho' so many Thousand labouring People have been imported.

9. The Danger therefore of these Colonies interfering with their Mother Country in Trades that depend on Labour, Manufactures, &c. is too remote to require the Attention of Great-Britain.

10. But in Proportion to the Increase of the Colonies, a vast Demand is growing for British Manufactures, a glorious Market wholly in the Power of Britain, in which Foreigners cannot interfere, which will increase in a short Time even beyond her Power of supplying, tho' her whole Trade should be to her Colonies: Therefore Britain should not too much restrain Manufactures in her Colonies. A wise and good Mother will not do it. To distress, is to weaken, and weakening the Children, weakens the whole Family. . . .

12. 'Tis an ill-grounded Opinion that by the Labour of Slaves, America may possibly vie in Cheapness of Manufactures with Britain. The Labour of Slaves can never be so cheap here as the Labour of working Men is in Britain. Any one may compute it. Interest of Money is in the Colonies from 6 to 10 per Cent. Slaves one with another cost £30 Sterling per Head. Reckon then

Source: Leonard W. Labaree, ed., *The Papers of Benjamin Franklin*, vol. 4 (New Haven, CT: Yale University Press, 1961), 225–34.

the Interest of the first Purchase of a Slave, the Insurance or Risque on his Life, his Cloathing and Diet, Expences in his Sickness and Loss of Time, Loss by his Neglect of Business (Neglect is natural to the Man who is not to be benefited by his own Care or Diligence), Expence of a Driver to keep him at Work, and his Pilfering from Time to Time, almost every Slave being *by Nature* a Thief, and compare the whole Amount with the Wages of a Manufacturer of Iron or Wool in England, you will see that Labour is much cheaper there than it ever can be by Negroes here. Why then will Americans purchase Slaves? Because Slaves may be kept as long as a Man pleases, or has Occasion for their Labour; while hired Men are continually leaving their Master (often in the midst of his Business,) and setting up for themselves.

13. As the Increase of People depends on the Encouragement of Marriages, the following Things must diminish a Nation, viz. 1. The being conquered; for the Conquerors will engross as many Offices, and exact as much Tribute or Profit on the Labour of the conquered, as will maintain them in their new Establishment, and this diminishing the Subsistence of the Natives discourages their Marriages, and so gradually diminishes them, while the Foreigners increase. 2. Loss of Territory. Thus the Britons being driven into Wales, and crowded together in a barren Country insufficient to support such great Numbers, diminished 'till the People bore a Proportion to the Produce, while the Saxons increas'd on their abandoned Lands; 'till the Island became full of English. And were the English now driven into Wales by some foreign Nation, there would in a few Years be no more Englishmen in Britain, than there are now People in Wales. 3. Loss of Trade. Manufactures exported, draw Subsistence from Foreign Countries for Numbers; who are thereby enabled to marry and raise Families. If the Nation be deprived of any Branch of Trade, and no new Employment is found for the People occupy'd in that Branch, it will also be soon deprived of so many People. 4. Loss of Food. Suppose a Nation has a Fishery, which not only employs great Numbers, but makes the Food and Subsistence of the People cheaper; If another Nation becomes Master of the Seas, and prevents the Fishery, the People will diminish in Proportion as the Loss of Employ, and Dearness of Provision, makes it more difficult to subsist a Family. 5. Bad Government and insecure Property. People not only leave such a Country,

and settling Abroad incorporate with other Nations, lose their native Language, and become Foreigners; but the Industry of those that remain being discourag'd, the Quantity of Subsistence in the Country is lessen'd, and the Support of a Family becomes more difficult. So heavy Taxes tend to diminish a People. . . . 6. The Introduction of Slaves. The Negroes brought into the English Sugar Islands, have greatly diminish'd the Whites there; the Poor are by this Means depriv'd of Employment, while a few Families acquire vast Estates; which they spend on Foreign Luxuries, and educating their Children in the Habit of those Luxuries; the same Income is needed for the Support of one that might have maintain'd 100. The Whites who have Slaves, not labouring, are enfeebled, and therefore not so generally prolific; the Slaves being work'd too hard, and ill fed, their Constitutions are broken, and the Deaths among them are more than the Births; so that a continual Supply is needed from Africa. The Northern Colonies having few Slaves increase in Whites. Slaves also pejorate the Families that use them; the white Children become proud, disgusted with Labour, and being educated in Idleness, are rendered unfit to get a Living by Industry. . . .

21. The Importation of Foreigners into a Country that has as many Inhabitants as the present Employments and Provisions for Subsistence will bear; will be in the End no Increase of People; unless the New Comers have more Industry and Frugality than the Natives, and then they will provide more Subsistence, and increase in the Country; but they will gradually eat the Natives out. Nor is it necessary to bring in Foreigners to fill up any occasional Vacancy in a Country; for such Vacancy (if the Laws are good, § 14, 16) will soon be filled by natural Generation. Who can now find the Vacancy made in Sweden, France or other Warlike Nations, by the Plague of Heroism 40 Years ago; in France, by the Expulsion of the Protestants; in England, by the Settlement of her Colonies; or in Guinea, by 100 Years Exportation of Slaves, that has blacken'd half America? The thinness of Inhabitants in Spain is owing to National Pride and Idleness, and other Causes, rather than to the Expulsion of the Moors, or to the making of new Settlements.

22. There is in short, no Bound to the prolific Nature of Plants or Animals, but what is made by their crowding and interfering with each others Means of

Subsistence. Was the Face of the Earth vacant of other Plants, it might be gradually sowed and overspread with one Kind only; as, for Instance, with Fennel; and were it empty of other Inhabitants, it might in a few Ages be replenish'd from one Nation only; as, for Instance, with Englishmen. Thus there are suppos'd to be now upwards of One Million English Souls in North-America, (tho' 'tis thought scarce 80,000 have been brought over Sea) and yet perhaps there is not one the fewer in Britain, but rather many more, on Account of the Employment the Colonies afford to Manufacturers at Home. This Million doubling, suppose but once in 25 Years, will in another Century be more than the People of England, and the greatest Number of Englishmen will be on this Side the Water. What an Accession of Power to the British Empire by Sea as well as Land! What Increase of Trade and Navigation! What Numbers of Ships and Seamen! We have been here but little more than 100 Years, and yet the Force of our Privateers in the late War, united, was greater, both in Men and Guns, than that of the whole British Navy in Queen Elizabeth's Time. How important an Affair then to Britain, is the present Treaty for settling the Bounds between her Colonies and the French, and how careful should she be to secure Room enough, since on the Room depends so much the Increase of her People?

23. . . . And since Detachments of English from Britain sent to America, will have their Places at Home so soon supply'd and increase so largely here; why should the Palatine Boors be suffered to swarm into our Settlements, and by herding together establish their Language and Manners to the Exclusion of ours? Why should Pennsylvania, founded by the English, become a Colony of *Aliens,* who will shortly be so numerous as to Germanize us instead of our Anglifying them, and will never adopt our Language or Customs, any more than they can acquire our Complexion.

24. Which leads me to add one Remark: That the Number of purely white People in the World is proportionably very small. All Africa is black or tawny. Asia chiefly tawny. America (exclusive of the new Comers) wholly so. And in Europe, the Spaniards, Italians, French, Russians and Swedes, are generally of what we call a swarthy Complexion; as are the Germans also, the Saxons only excepted, who with the English, make the principal Body of White People on the Face of the Earth. I could wish their Numbers were increased. And while we are, as I may call it, *Scouring* our Planet, by clearing America of Woods, and so making this Side of our Globe reflect a brighter Light to the Eyes of Inhabitants in Mars or Venus, why should we in the Sight of Superior Beings, darken its People? why increase the Sons of Africa, by Planting them in America, where we have so fair an Opportunity, by excluding all Blacks and Tawneys, of increasing the lovely White and Red? But perhaps I am partial to the Complexion of my Country, for such Kind of Partiality is natural to Mankind.

QUESTIONS

1. What were Franklin's views on slavery? In what ways do these views resemble those of the editors of the *Boston News-Letter* (Reading 4.1)? In what ways do his views on slavery differ from those expressed in that document?

2. Why did Franklin take such a dim view of German immigration?

3. How does his opposition to German immigration and slavery relate to his case for a more prominent role for colonists within the British Empire?

5.5. DIARY OF HANNAH HEATON, EXCERPTS FROM HER RECOLLECTIONS OF THE GREAT AWAKENING (1750s)

Sometime in the 1750s, after she had married and resettled on a farm in North Haven, Connecticut, Hannah Heaton began to keep a diary in which she occasionally commented on her spiritual experiences and significant events such as the American Revolution. It seems that Heaton primarily saw the diary as a way to record and sustain her spiritual development. Later, she also came to view it as a way to instruct her children and have them remember her. Below are excerpts of Heaton's recollections of her conversion during the Great Awakening when she was 20 years old.

Now after a while i went over to new haven in the fall just before that great work of god began which was in the year 1741. There i heard mr tennant and mr whitefeild preach which awakened me much. Mr whitefeild laid down the marks of an unconverted person. O strange it was such preaching as i never heard before. Dont you said he when you are at the house of god long service should be over that your minds may be about your worldly conserns and pleasures. Is it not a wearines to you said he if one days serving god is so wearisom to you. How could you endure to be in heaven with him forever where nothing but praises are. He said if you was carried to heaven in this condition the first prayer you would make would be that yould might go into hell for that would be more agreeable to your natures. O thot i i have found it a wearines to me many a time over and over again. Then i began to think my nature must be changed but how to attain it i knew not. When i was coming from meeting to my quarters which was about 6 miles my company began to worry me to sing. I put them of till i feard they would be offended. . . . . I thot that was better than to sing a song but o they little thot how i felt. It was hard work for me to sing i felt in such distress in my mind but i went to frollicks all winter and stifeld the conviction i had of its being a soul ruining sin. I was much for fine cloaths and fashons. In the spring in may i went to middletown to keep election. One of the days while i was there i was at a tavern in a frolick. Then there come in a young man from long island belonging to the society that i did and told me how the work of god was carried on there and of several of my mates that was converted. My sister elisabeth also sent a letter. I trembled when i read it. She said her soul magnifyed the lord her spirit rejoysed in god her saviour. Her sighs was turned into songs the comforter is come. I had a strong impression upon my mind to go home which i did in a few days. As soon as i got into my fathers house young people come in and began to talk. Sister elisabeth began to cry over me because i had no intrest in christ. That i wonderd at but the next morning father examined me and i was forst to tell my experiences as wel as i could. He told me when i had done what a dreadful condition i was in. It took hold of my heart. I kept going to the meetings and was more and more concerned. And o what crying out there was among the people what shall i do to be saved. . . . O how i did invi toads or any creature that had no souls to perish eternally. Many a time i kneeled down to pray and my mouth was as it were stopt and i did vent out my anguish with tears and groans and a

Source: Barbara E. Lacey, ed., *The World of Hannah Heaton: The Diary of an Eighteenth-Century New England Farm Woman* (DeKalb, Ill.: Northern Illinois University Press, 2003), 6–9.

few broken speches. Now it cut me to think how i had spent my precious time in vanity and sin against god. My not regarding the sabbath no more was bitter to me now. . . . O how it cut me to think i could not get away from god but appear before him i must and i lived in daily expectation of it. Now sometimes it would be cast into my mind thus you need not be so conserned you are not so great a sinner as some are some have murdered and done dreadful things but you pray and go to meeting and god will not have a heart to send you to hell. This i thot was the devil trying to beat me of. . . .

I was such a loathsome sinner and he such a holy god sometimes i thot i was willing but he was not. I could hear of others finding mercy but o how it would strike me for i feard greatly that while others was taken i should be left. Now the promises in the schriptures was terror to me for i thot they belonged to the children of god. I had no part in them and i felt such an enmity against the way of salvation by christ. I could see no way to escape damnation. Now i began to feel like one lost in the woods. I knew not what to do nor what course to take for my heart began to grow hard. Now i could not cry and pray as before when i thot of hell. It did not terrify me as before it use to. Me thot i envied the very devils for they believed and trembled but i did not. Nothing now semd to help me. I grew worse and worse. . . . I thot it must be a gone case with me and i thot so the more because father never spoke one word to me about my soul in particular as i remember after he first examined me till after i had found comfort which was about three weeaks after. It being in the year 1741 june 20 i was then i suppose in my twentieth year. It was the lord's day. I went to our separate meeting in the school house. . . .

Meeting being done i got away to go home. I thot i would not go to the night meeting which was to be at thomas sanfords for it would do me no good. I remember in the lot as i went i see strawberries and these thots past through my mind. I may as wel go to picking strawberries now as not its no matter what i do its a gone case with me. I fear i have committed the unpardonable sin and now herdned but as i was going home i considered at last. I turned and went to meeting. Soon after meeting began the power of god come down. Many were crying out the other side of the room what shall i do to be saved. I was immediately moved to pres through the multitude and went to them. A great melting of soul come up on me. I wept bitterly and pleaded hard for mercy mercy. Now i was brought to vew the justice of god due to me for my sin. It made me tremble my knees smote together then i thot of belshezer when he see the hand writing against him. It seemd to me i was a sinking down into hell. I thot the flor i stood on gave way and i was just a going but then i began to resign and as i resind my distres began to go of till i was perfectly easy quiet and calm. I could say lord it is just if i sink in to hell. I felt for a few moments like a creature dead. I was nothing i could do nothing nor i desired nothing. I had not so much as one desire for mercy left me but presently i heard one in the room say seek and you shall find come to me all you that are weary and heavy laden and i will give you rest. I began to feel a thirsting after christ and began to beg for mercy free mercy for jesus sake. Me thot i see jesus with the eyes of my soul stand up in heaven. A lovely god man with his arms open ready to receive me his face was full of smiles he lookt white and ruddy and was just such a saviour as my soul wanted every way suitable for me. O how it melted my heart to think he had been willing all this while to save me but i was not willing which i never believed before now. I cryed from the very heart to think what a tender herted savior i had been refusing how often i turned a deaf ear to his gracious calls and invitations. All that had kept me from him was my will. Jesus appeared altogether lovely to me now.

My heart went out with love and thankfulness and admiration. I cryed why me lord and leave so many. O what a fulnes was their in christ for others if they would come and give up their all to him. I went about the room and invited people to come to him.

QUESTIONS

1. What, according to Heaton, prompted her conversion?
2. What did Heaton's conversion mean to her?
3. Based on Heaton's description, what was it like to live in New England during the Great Awakening? How did neighbors and family members experience and discuss religion?

CHAPTER 6

EMPIRE AND RESISTANCE, 1763 TO 1776

6.1. KING CHARLES III OF SPAIN, APPOINTMENT OF JOSÉ DE GÁLVEZ AS VISITOR GENERAL TO NEW SPAIN (1765)

Charles III, in appointing José de Gálvez as Visitor General, gave him great authority to inspect financial, judicial, and governmental matters in New Spain. Gálvez's main assignment was to improve the flow of revenues from the colonies to Spain, but these instructions also granted him enough power to accomplish other colonial goals, such as the expansion of settlement in North America and the expulsion of the Jesuits from New Spain.

Instruction Reservada, March 14, 1765

The King: Don Joseph Galvez, of my Council, *Alcalde de mi Casa y Corte*, and honorary minister with seniority of the Council of the Indies; notwithstanding that I am well satisfied with the zeal, activity, prudence, and disinterest with which the branches and revenues of my royal patrimony are managed by my viceroy of New Spain and by the ministers of my real hacienda, the governors, and other subordinates who serve under their orders, it being necessary, on account of the large sums needed in attending to the obligations of my royal crown, to exhaust all means from the revenues to the end that the burden of imposing new contributions may be avoided, and to collect all legitimate

duties as legally provided without altering established practice or dispensing voluntary favors, and to prevent abuses and all superfluous expenses not absolutely indispensable for the best administration of revenues:

I have deemed it convenient to my royal service to name you, Don Joseph Galvez—a minister in whom I have entire satisfaction and confidence, able, zealous, and skilled in the management of revenues—that you may, in the capacity of visitor-general to my real hacienda within the jurisdiction of the kingdom of New Spain, take cognizance of all of them, examine their proceeds, expenses, balances, and the whereabouts of their funds; demand any arrears in which the administrators, treasurers, lessees of revenues, or other persons who have managed rents, may be to my real hacienda;

Source: Herbert Ingram Priestley, *José De Gálvez, Visitor-General of New Spain (1765–1771)* (Berkeley: University of California Press, 1916), 404.

and regulate the system and management with which the revenues are to be administered in future, reducing expenses and salaries which can and ought to be lowered or abolished, so that the balances be not dissipated by unnecessary expense, but made more effective to their destined ends.

I grant you for all this, and for all that is to be expressed, the powers and jurisdiction which you need to give your commission entire fulfillment. To this end I desire that my viceroy and captain-general of New Spain shall take all measures which you ask and give you the assistance you need. . . .

QUESTIONS

1. How did Charles III expect Gálvez to raise royal revenues in New Spain?
2. What kind of power does this set of instructions grant to Gálvez?
3. How did Charles III express his kingly authority in this proclamation?

6.2. WILLIAM PITT, *OPPOSING THE STAMP ACT IN PARLIAMENT* (1766)

Whig politician William Pitt spoke out strongly in the House of Commons against the Stamp Act in two speeches on January 14, 1766. Pitt thought taxing American colonists violated the concept of British liberty, but he did not support the idea that North American colonies should be independent of British control.

As to the late ministry [turning to Grenville who sat near him], every capital measure they have taken has been entirely wrong. . . . The manner in which this affair will be terminated will decide the judgment of posterity on the glory of this kingdom and the wisdom of its government during the present reign. . . . On a question that may mortally wound the freedom of three millions of virtuous and brave subjects beyond the Atlantic Ocean, I cannot be silent. . . . It is my opinion that this kingdom has no right to lay a tax upon the colonies. At the same time, I assert the authority of this kingdom over the colonies to be sovereign and supreme, in every circumstance of government and legislation whatsoever. They are the subjects of this kingdom, equally entitled with yourselves to all the natural rights of mankind, and the peculiar privileges of Englishmen: equally bound by its laws and equally participating of the constitution of this free country. The Americans are the sons, not the bastards of England. As subjects they are entitled to the common right of representation and cannot be bound to pay taxes without their consent.

Taxation is no part of the governing power. The taxes are a voluntary gift and grant of the Commons alone...when therefore in this House we give and grant, we give what is our own. But in an American tax what do we do? We your Majesty's Commons of Great Britain give and grant to your Majesty—what? Our own property? No. We give and grant to your Majesty the property of your Majesty's Commons in America. It is an absurdity of terms. . . .

The Commons of America represented in their several assemblies have ever been in possession of this their constitutional right of giving and granting their

Source: Basil Williams, *The Life of William Pitt, Earl of Chatham*, Vol. II (New York: Longmans, Green, & Co., 1914), 191–2, 195, googlebooks.com

own money. They would have been slaves if they had not enjoyed it. . . . If this House suffers the Stamp Act to continue in force, France will gain more by your colonies than she ever could have done if her arms in the last war had been victorious. . . .

[Pitt later rose and spoke again in the same debate]. America is almost in open rebellion. I rejoice that America has resisted. . . .

Upon the whole, I will beg leave to tell the House what is really my opinion. It is, that the Stamp Act be repealed absolutely, totally, and immediately; that the reason for the repeal should be assigned, because it was founded on an erroneous principle. At the same time, let the sovereign authority of this country over the colonies be asserted in as strong terms as can be devised, and be made to extend every point of legislation whatsoever: that we may bind their trade, confine their manufactures, and exercise every power whatsoever—except that of taking money out of their pockets without their consent.

QUESTIONS

1. Why did Pitt argue that the colonists should be taxed by Parliament?
2. Pitt argued that Britain had "sovereign and supreme" authority over the colonies. How did he reconcile this with opposing the Stamp Act?
3. According to Pitt, who could tax the American colonists?

6.3. JOHN DICKINSON, "THE LIBERTY SONG" (1768)

John Dickinson published these song lyrics, meant to be sung to the British tune "Heart of Oak," in the *Boston Gazette* in July 1768 and then in the *Boston Chronicle* on August 29, 1768. This song was one of many that were sung in the colonies during popular protests against the British. The appearance of song lyrics in newspapers could also cement allegiance to the cause, and printed lyrics could be posted in public places, such as taverns, to rouse public support. Protest songs were also used as drinking songs to accompany toasts at political gatherings. This song references a "bumper," a glass full of alcohol that is raised in a toast.

The LIBERTY Song
COME join hand in hand brave AMERICANS all,
And rouse your bold hearts at fair LIBERTY's call;
No tyrannous acts shall suppress your just claim
Or stain with dishonor AMERICA'S name
   In FREEDOM we're born—Let's give them a
      cheer—
   Our purses are ready
   Steady, Friends, steady,
   Not as SLAVES, but as FREEMEN our Money
      we'll give . . .

Then join Hand in Hand brave AMERICANS all,
By uniting we stand, by dividing we fall;
In so RIGHTEOUS a Cause let us hope to succeed,
For Heaven approves of each generous Deed.
   In FREEDOM we're born, etc.
All Ages shall speak with Amaze and Applause,
Of the Courage we'll shew in support of our
     LAWS;
To die we can bear—but to serve we disdain.
For Shame is to FREEDOM more dreadful than
   pain

Source: Boston Chronicle, August 29–September 5, 1768.

In FREEDOM we're born, etc.
This Bumper I crown for our Sovereign's Health,
And this for Britannia's Glory and wealth;
That Wealth and that glory immortal may be,
If she is but JUST—and if we are but FREE
    IN FREEDOM we're born, and in FREEDOM
        we'll live
    Our purses are ready,
    Steady, Friends, steady
    Not as SLAVES but as FREEMEN our Money
        we'll give.

QUESTIONS

1. How does this song define freedom and slavery?
2. Why would protestors who sang this song be willing to toast to King George III and "Britainnia's Glory" while simultaneously resisting "tyrannous" Parliamentary taxes?
3. Do you think a song like this could convince anyone to join the Non-Importation Movement?

6.4. THOMAS HUTCHINSON, EXCERPTS FROM LETTERS TO GREAT BRITAIN DESCRIBING POPULAR UNREST (1768, 1769)

Thomas Hutchinson, a native of Massachusetts who served as the colony's lieutenant governor and chief justice, found himself facing the wrath of protesters during the imperial crisis of the 1760s. His house was demolished by a mob protesting his proposed enforcement of the Stamp Act in 1765. In this letter from 1768, he describes riots in Boston to authorities in Great Britain and worries about resistance in the event that British troops were housed with Boston residents.

Principles of government absurd enough spread thro' all the colonies; but I cannot think that in any colony, people of any consideration have ever been so mad as to think of a revolt. Many of the common people have been in a frenzy, and talk'd of dying in defence of their liberties, and have spoke and printed what is highly criminal, and too many of rank above the vulgar, and some *in public posts* have countenanced and encouraged them until they increased so much in their numbers and opinion of their importance as to submit to government no further than they have thought proper. The legislative powers have been influenced by them, and the executive powers intirely lost their force. . . . For four or five weeks past the distemper has been growing, and I confess I have been without some apprehensions for myself, but my friends had more for me. . . .

The last spring there had been several riots, and a most infamous libel had been published in one of the papers. . . . Whilst we were in this state, news came of two regiments being ordered from Halifax, and soon after two more from Ireland. The minds of the people were more and more agitated, broad hints were given that the troops should never land, a barrel of tar was placed upon the beacon, in the night to be fired to bring in the country when the government troops appeared, and all the authority of the government was not strong enough to remove it. The town of Boston met and passed a number of weak but very criminal votes. . . .

Source: Copy of Letters Sent to Great Britain, by His Excellency Thomas Hutchinson, the Hon. Andrew Oliver, and Several Other Persons, Born and Educated among Us (Boston: Edes and Gill, 1773), 9–12, 16.

In this confusion the troops from Halifax arrived. I never was much afraid of the people's taking arms, but I was apprehensive of violence from the mob, it being their last chance before the troops could land. As the prospect of revenge became more certain their courage abated in proportion. Two regiments are landed, but a new grievance is now rais'd. The troops are by act of parliament to be quartered no where else but in the barracks untill they are full. There are barracks enough at the castle to hold both regiments. . . .

The government has been so long in the hands of the populace that it must come out of them by degrees, at least it will be a work of time to bring the people back to just notions of the nature of government.

[In another letter from January 1769, Hutchinson appealed for more help to put down unrest in Boston. His letters were meant to be private, but copies were published in 1773, after Hutchinson had been appointed royal governor. They seriously damaged his reputation, and he fled to England after the American Revolution broke out.]

This is most certainly a crisis. I really wish that there may not have been the least degree of severity beyond what is absolutely necessary to maintain, I think I may say to you the *dependance* [sic] which a colony ought to have upon the parent state; but if no measures shall have been taken to secure this dependance, or nothing more than some declaratory acts or resolves, *it is all over with us.* . . .

There must be an abridgment of what are called English liberties. I relieve myself by considering that in a remove from the state of nature to the most perfect state of government there must be a great restraint of liberty. I doubt whether it is possible to project a system of government in which a colony 3000 miles distant from the parent state shall enjoy all the liberty of the parent state. . . . I wish the good of the colony when I wish to see some further restraint of liberty rather than the connexion with the parent state should be broken; for I am sure such a breach must prove the ruin of the colony.

QUESTIONS

1. How does Hutchinson characterize the actions of people from different social classes?
2. How does Hutchinson think the colonial unrest should be controlled?
3. Why did the publication of these letters contribute to Hutchinson's disgrace and exile?

6.5. ABIGAIL ADAMS, EXCERPTS FROM LETTERS TO JOHN ADAMS ABOUT THE BATTLE OF BUNKER HILL AND CONDITIONS IN BOSTON (1775)

Abigail Adams wrote several letters to her husband, John Adams, who was serving in the Continental Congress, to tell him about the Battle of Bunker Hill, which she had witnessed from across the Charles River. In the excerpts below, she reports on the death of Dr. Joseph Warren, a strong patriot who became known as the primary hero of Bunker Hill.

Source: Charles Francis Adams, ed., *Letters of Mrs. Adams* (Boston: Charles C. Little and James Brown, 1840), 39–40, 49, 52–53.

Sunday, 18 June, 1775

The day,—perhaps, the decisive day,—is come, on which the fate of America depends. My bursting heart must find vent at my pen. I have just heard, that our dear friend, Dr. Warren, is no more, but fell gloriously fighting for his country; saying, better to die honorably in the field, than ignominiously hang upon the gallows. Great is our loss. He has distinguished himself in every engagement, by his courage and fortitude, by animating the soldiers, and leading them on by his own example. A particular account of these dreadful, but I hope glorious days will be transmitted you, no doubt, in the exactest manner. . . .

Charlestown is laid in ashes. The battle began upon our intrenchments upon Bunker's Hill, Saturday morning about three o'clock, and has not cased yet, and it is now three o'clock Sabbath afternoon.

It is expected they will come out over the Neck tonight, and a dreadful battle must ensue. Almighty God, cover the heads of our countrymen, and be a shield to our dear friends! How many have fallen, we know not. The constant roar of the cannon is so distressing, that we cannot eat, drink, or sleep. May we be supported and sustained in the dreadful conflict. I shall tarry here till it is thought unsafe by my friends, and then I have secured myself a retreat at your brother's, who has kindly offered me part of his house. I cannot compose myself to write any further at present. I will add more as I hear further. . . .

5 July, 1775

I would not have you be distressed about me. Danger, they say, makes people valiant. I have been distressed, but not dismayed. I have felt for my country and her sons, and have bled with them and for them. Not all the havoc and devastation they have made, has wounded me like the death of Warren. We want him in the Senate; we want him in his profession; we want him in the field. We mourn for the citizen, the senator, the physician, and the warrior. May we have others raised up in his room.

16 July, 1775

The appointments of the generals Washington and Lee gives universal satisfaction. . . . I was struck with General Washington. You had prepared me to entertain a favorable opinion of him, but I thought the half was not told me. Dignity with ease and complacency, the gentleman and the soldier, look agreeably blended in him. . . .

As to intelligence from Boston . . . I heard yesterday, by one Mr. Roulstone, a goldsmith, who got out in a fishing schooner, that their distress increased upon them fast. Their beef is all spent; their malt and cider all gone. All the fresh provisions they can procure, they are obliged to give to the sick and wounded. . . . No man dared now to be seen talking to his friend in the street. They were obliged to be within, every evening, at ten o'clock, according to martial law; nor could any inhabitant walk any street in town after that time, without a pass from [British commander] Gage. He has ordered all the molasses to be distilled up into rum for the soldiers. . . .

Every article here in the West India way is very scarce and dear. In six weeks we shall not be able to purchase any article of the kind. I wish you would let Bass get me one pound of pepper, and two yards of black calamanco for shoes. . . . You can hardly imagine how much we want many common small articles, which are not manufactured amongst ourselves; but we will have them in time; not one pin to be purchased for love or money.

QUESTIONS

1. What qualities does Adams admire in patriots and military leaders?

2. What evidence do these letters offer regarding women's roles in the American Revolution?

3. How was the beginning of the Revolutionary War altering the everyday life of Abigail Adams?

CHAPTER 7

A REVOLUTIONARY NATION, 1776 TO 1789

7.1 VISUAL DOCUMENT: PIERRE LE BEAU, PORTRAIT OF BENJAMIN FRANKLIN (1780s)

Pierre Le Beau engraved this portrait of Benjamin Franklin after a portrait by Claude Desrais, and it was published in Paris in the 1780s. The caption notes that Franklin was "born in Boston in New England on 17 January 1706." The artist depicts Franklin in the

Source: Courtesy of the Library of Congress Prints and Photographs Division, LC-USZ62-28230.

fur hat that he was fond of wearing in Paris to portray himself as a "rustic" American. He is not wearing his trademark spectacles in this portrait, but his famous face would have been very recognizable to Parisians nonetheless. This engraving is typical of the scores of Franklin portraits that Parisians reproduced on paper, candy boxes, ceramics, and other items in the 1780s.

QUESTIONS

1. Why would Parisians want to buy an engraving of Franklin like this one?

2. How does Franklin's appearance in this image communicate a message about his reputation?

3. Why use an engraving of Franklin to popularize him in France, rather than a written document?

7.2. DIARY OF SURGEON ALBIGENCE WALDO, EXCERPTS DESCRIBING THE CONTINENTAL ARMY'S ENCAMPMENT AT VALLEY FORGE (1777)

Albigence Waldo was a physician from Pomfret, Connecticut, who served as a surgeon with the First Connecticut Infantry Regiment, a militia unit that joined the Continental Army in Pennsylvania in September 1777. Waldo's diary entries about the Continental Army's winter quarters in Valley Forge, Pennsylvania, at the end of 1777 paint a harrowing picture of the conditions that soldiers there faced.

Dec. 12th [1777].—A Bridge of Waggons made across the Schuylkill last Night consisting of 36 waggons, with a bridge of Rails between each. . . . Militia and dragoons brought into Camp several Prisoners. Sun Set.—We are order'd to march over the River—It snows—I'm Sick—eat nothing—No Whiskey—No Forage—Lord—Lord—Lord. The Army were 'till Sun Rise crossing the River—some at the Waggon Bridge, & some at the Raft Bridge below. Cold & uncomfortable.

Dec. 13th—The army march'd three miles from the West side the River and encamp'd near a place call'd the Gulph and not an improper name neither, for this Gulph seems well adapted by its situation to keep us from the pleasure & enjoyments of this World, or being conversant with any body in it. . . .

Dec. 14th—Prisoners & Deserters are continually coming in. The Army which has been surprisingly healthy hitherto, now begin to grow sickly from the continued fatigues they have suffered this Campaign. Yet they still show spirit of Alacrity & Contentment not to be expected from so young Troops. I am Sick—discontented—out of humour. Poor food—hard lodging—Cold Water—fatigue—Nasty Cloaths—nasty Cookery—Vomit half my time—smoak'd out of my senses—the Devil's in't—I can't Endure it—Why are we sent here to starve and freeze—What sweet Felicities have I left at home; A charming Wife—pretty Children—Good Beds—good food—good Cookery—all agreeable—all harmonious. Here all Confusion—smoke Cold—hunger & filthyness—A pox on my

Source: "Diary of Surgeon Albigence Waldo, of the Connecticut Line," *Pennsylvania Magazine of History and Biography* 21 (1897): 305–09.

bad luck. There comes a bowl of beef soup—full of burnt leaves and dirt, sickish enough to make a hector spue,—away with it Boys—I'll live like a Chameleon upon Air. . . . See the poor Soldier, when in health—with what cheerfulness he meets his foes and encounters every hardship—if barefoot, he labours thro' the Mud & Cold with a Song in his mouth extolling War & Washington—if his food be bad, he eats it notwithstanding with seeming content—blesses God for a good Stomach and Whistles it into digestion. But harkee Patience, a moment—There comes a Soldier, his bare feet are seen thro' his worn out Shoes, his legs nearly naked from the tatter'd remains of an only pair of stockings, his Breeches not sufficient to cover his nakedness, his Shirt hanging in Strings, his hair dishevell'd, his face meager; his whole appearance pictures a person forsaken & discouraged. He comes, and crys with an air of wretchedness & despair, I am Sick, my feet lame, my legs are sore, my body cover'd with this tormenting Itch—my Cloaths are worn out, my Constitution is broken, my former Activity is exhausted by fatigue, hunger & Cold, I fail fast I shall soon be no more! And all the reward I shall get will be—"Poor Will is dead!" People who live at home in Luxury and Ease, quietly possessing their habitations, Enjoying their Wives & families in peace, have but a very faint Idea of the unpleasing sensations, and continual Anxiety the Man endures who is in a Camp,

and is the husband and parent of an agreeable family. These same People are willing we should suffer every thing for their Benefit & advantage, and yet are the first to Condemn us for not doing more!! . . .

Dec. 21st—Preparations made for hutts. Provision Scarce. Mr. Ellis went homeward—sent a Letter to my Wife. Heartily wish myself at home—my Skin & eyes are almost spoil'd with continual smoke.

A general cry thro' the camp this Evening among the Soldiers, "No Meat! No Meat!"—the Distant vales Echo'd back the melancholly sound—"No Meat! No Meat!" Immitating the noise of Crows & Owls, also, made a part of the confused Musick.

What have you for our Dinners Boys? "Nothing but Fire Cake & Water, Sir." At night, "Gentlemen the Supper is ready." What is your supper, Lads? "Fire Cake & Water, Sir." Very poor beef has been drawn in our Camp the greater part of this season.

QUESTIONS

1. How did his experience at Valley Forge give Waldo a sense of how military men are separated from civilians?
2. What were the causes of suffering at Valley Forge?
3. How does Waldo's experience help us to understand the relationship between morale and politics in the Revolutionary military?

7.3 BOSTON KING, EXCERPTS FROM "MEMOIRS OF THE LIFE OF BOSTON KING: A BLACK PREACHER" (1798)

In his memoir, Boston King describes escaping from slavery to fight with the British in 1780 and his subsequent attempts to keep his freedom. The British moved King to Nova Scotia after the war, and he later emigrated to Sierra Leone with his family.

Source: Boston King, "Memoirs of the Life of Boston King: A Black Preacher (1798)," in *If We Must Die: African American Voices on War and Peace*, ed. Karin L. Stanford (New York: Rowman & Littlefield, 2008), 21–23.

My master being apprehensive that Charles-Town was in danger on account of the war, removed into the country, about 38 miles off. Here we built a large house for Mr. Waters, during which time the English took Charles-Town. . . . To escape his cruelty, I determined to go to Charles-Town, and throw myself into the hands of the English. They received me readily, and I began to feel the happiness of liberty, of which I knew nothing before, altho' I was much grieved at first, to be obliged to leave my friends, and reside among strangers. In this situation I was seized with small-pox, and suffered great hardships; for all the Blacks affected with that disease, were ordered to be carried a mile from the camp, lest the soldiers should be infected, and disabled from marching. . . .

Being recovered, I marched with the army to Chamblem. . . . From thence I went to a place about 35 miles off, where we stayed two months: at the expiration of which, an express came to the Colonel to decamp in fifteen minutes. When these orders arrived I was at a distance from the camp, catching some fish for the captain that I waited upon; upon returning to the camp, to my great astonishment, I found all the English were gone, and had left only a few militia. I felt my mind greatly alarmed, but Captain Lewes, who commanded the militia, said, "You need not be uneasy, for you will see your regiment before 7 o'clock tonight." This satisfied me for the present, and in two hours we set off.

As [we] were on the march, the Captain asked, "How will you like me to be your master?"

I answered, that I was Captain Grey's servant. "Yes," said he; "but I expect that they are all taken prisoners before now; and I have been long enough in the English service, and am determined to leave them." These words roused my indignation, and I spoke some sharp words to him. But he calmly replied, "If you do not behave well, I will put you in irons, and give you a dozen stripes every morning." I now perceived that my case was desperate, and that I had nothing to trust

to, but to wait the first opportunity for making my escape. . . .

I tarried with Captain Grey about a year, and then left him, and came to Nelson's-ferry. Here I entered into the service of the commanding officer of that place. But our situation was very precarious, and we expected to be made prisoners every day; for the Americans had 1600 men, not far off; whereas our whole number amounted only to 250: But there were 1200 English about 30 miles off; only we knew not how to inform him of our danger, as the Americans were in possession of the country. Our commander at length determined to send me with a letter, promising me great rewards, if I was successful in the business. . . .

Soon after I went to Charles-Town, and entered on board a man of war. As we were going to Chesapeak-bay, we were at the taking of a rich prize. We stayed in the bay two days, and then sailed for New-York, where we went on shore. Here I endeavored to follow my trade, but for want of tools was obliged to relinquish it, and enter service. . . . I then went out on a pilot-boat. We were at sea eight days, and had only provisions for five, so that we were in danger of starving. On the 9th day we were taken by an American whale-boat. I went on board them with a cheerful countenance, and asked for bread and water, and made very free with them . . . my mind was sorely distressed at the thought of being again reduced to slavery, and separated from my wife and family; and at the same time it was exceeding difficult to escape from my bondage. . . .

[In 1783] the horrors and devastation of war happily terminated, and peace was restored between America and Great Britain, which diffused universal joy among all parties, except us, who had escaped from slavery, and taken refuge in the English army; for a report prevailed at New-York, that all the slaves, in number 2000, were to be delivered up to their masters, altho' some of them had been three or four years among the English. . . . The English had compassion upon us in the day of distress, and issued out the Proc-lamation, importing, That all slaves should be free, who had taken refuge in the British lines. . . . Each of us received a certificate from the commanding officer at New-York, which dispelled all our fears, and filled us with joy and gratitude. Soon after, ships were fitted out, and furnished with every necessary for conveying us to Nova Scotia.

1. King relates how he found "the happiness of lib-erty" for the first time after his escape from slavery. Of what did his sense of "liberty" consist?
2. How did King use different kinds of work and labor to maintain his freedom?
3. Why was King so happy to go to Nova Scotia at the end of the war?

7.4. JAMES MADISON, EXCERPTS FROM "FEDERALIST NO. 51" (1788)

James Madison published this essay in the *New York Packet* on February 8, 1788. He wrote anony-mously as "Publius" as part of the effort to convince the New York convention to ratify the U.S. Constitution. In this essay, Madison sought to reassure New Yorkers that the federal government would not grow too powerful.

To what expedient, then, shall we finally resort, for maintaining in practice the necessary partition of power among the several departments, as laid down in the Constitution? The only answer that can be given is . . . by so contriving the interior structure of the gov-ernment as that its several constituent parts may, by their mutual relations, be the means of keeping each other in their proper places. . . . In order to lay a due foundation for that separate and distinct exercise of the different powers of government, which to a certain extent is admitted on all hands to be essential to the preservation of liberty, it is evident that each depart-ment should have a will of its own; and consequently should be so constituted that the members of each should have as little agency as possible in the appoint-ment of the members of the others. Were this prin-ciple rigorously adhered to, it would require that all the appointments for the supreme executive, legisla-tive, and judiciary magistracies should be drawn from the same fountain of authority, the people, through

channels having no communication whatever with one another. . . .

It is equally evident, that the members of each department should be as little dependent as possible on those of the others, for the emoluments annexed to their offices. Were the executive magistrate, or the judges, not independent of the legislature in this par-ticular, their independence in every other would be merely nominal.

But the great security against a gradual concentra-tion of the several powers in the same department, consists in giving to those who administer each depart-ment the necessary constitutional means and personal motives to resist encroachments of the others. . . . Am-bition must be made to counteract ambition. The interest of the man must be connected with the con-stitutional rights of the place. It may be a reflection on human nature, that such devices should be neces-sary to control the abuses of government. But what is government itself, but the greatest of all reflections on

Source: The Federalist: A Commentary on The Constitution of the United States (New York: G. P. Putnam's Sons, 1888), 322–25.

human nature? If men were angels, no government would be necessary. If angels were to govern men, neither external nor internal controls on government would be necessary. In framing a government which is to be administered by men over men, the great difficulty lies in this: you must first enable the government to control the governed; and in the next place oblige it to control itself. A dependence on the people is, no doubt, the primary control on the government; but experience has taught mankind the necessity of auxiliary precautions. . . .

But it is not possible to give each department an equal power of self-defense. In republican government, the legislative authority necessarily predominates. The remedy for this inconveniency is to divide the legislature into different branches; and to render them, by different modes of election and different principles

of action, as little connected with each other as the nature of their common functions and their common dependence on society will admit. . . . The weakness of the executive may require, on the other hand, that it should be fortified.

QUESTIONS

1. How would keeping the powers of the branches of government separate help in "the preservation of liberty," according to Madison?

2. Why was the independence of the judicial and executive branches from the legislative branch so important to Madison?

3. What roles do "interest" and "ambition" play in controlling government power, according to Madison?

7.5. MERCY OTIS WARREN, *OBSERVATIONS ON THE NEW CONSTITUTION, AND THE FEDERAL AND STATE CONVENTIONS BY A COLUMBIAN PATRIOT* (1788)

This pamphlet, anonymously published by playwright and historian Mercy Otis Warren, criticized the proposed U.S. Constitution for proposing to consolidate too much centralized power in the federal government. Warren criticized the elitism and secrecy of the Constitutional Convention, and she called on the state ratifying conventions to reject the Constitution. Warren's fear of power and her conspiratorial tone were typical of many other Antifederalists.

Animated with the firmest zeal for the interest of this country, the peace and union of the American States, and the freedom and happiness of a people who have made the most costly sacrifices in the cause of liberty,—who have braved the power of Britain, weathered the convulsions of war, and waded thro' the blood of friends and foes to establish their independence and

to support the freedom of the human mind; I cannot silently witness this degradation without calling on them, before they are compelled to blush at their own servitude, and to turn back their languid eyes on their lost liberties. . . . Self defence is a primary law of nature, which no subsequent law of society can abolish; this primeval principle, the immediate gift of the

Source: "Observations on the New Constitution, and the Federal and State Conventions by a Columbian Patriot," in *An Additional Number of Letters from the Federal Farmer to the Republican*, reprint ed. (Chicago: Quadrangle Books, 1962).

Creator, obliges every one to remonstrate against the strides of ambition, and a wanton lust of domination, and to resist the first approaches of tyranny, which at this day threaten to sweep away the rights for which the brave sons of America have fought with an heroism scarcely paralleled even in ancient republicks. . . .

The mode in which this constitution is recommended to the people to judge without either the advice of Congress, or the legislatures of the several states, is very reprehensible—it is an attempt to force it upon them before it could be the roughly understood, and may leave us in that situation, that in the first moments of slavery the minds of the people agitated by the remembrance of their lost liberties, will be like the sea in a tempest, that sweeps down every mound of security.

But it is needless to enumerate other instances, in which the proposed constitution appears contradictory to the first principles which ought to govern mankind; and it is equally so to enquire into the motives that induced to so bold a step as the annihilation of the independence and sovereignty of the thirteen distinct states.—They are but too obvious through the whole progress of the business, from the first shutting up the doors of the federal convention and resolving that no member should correspond with gentlemen in the different states on the subject under discussion; till the trivial proposition of *recommending* a few amendments was artfully ushered into the convention of the Massachusetts. . . .

And the hurry with which it has been urged to the acceptance of the people, without giving time, by adjournments, for better information, and more unanimity has a deceptive appearance . . . may the people be calm, and wait a legal redress; may the mad transport of some of our infatuated capitals subside; and every influential character through the States, make the most prudent exertions for a new general Convention, who may vest adequate powers in Congress, for all national purposes, without annihilating the individual governments, and drawing blood from every pore by taxes, impositions and illegal restrictions—This step might again re-establish the Union, restore tranquility to the ruffled mind of the inhabitants, and save America from distresses dreadful even in contemplation. . . . Though several State Conventions have assented to, and ratified, yet the voice of the people appears at present strong against the adoption of the Constitution. . .—by the imbecility of some, and the duplicity of others, a majority of the Convention of Massachusetts have been flattered with the ideas of amendments, when it will be too late to complain.

QUESTIONS

1. How does Warren contend that the proposed constitution betrayed the legacy of the American Revolution?
2. What are Warren's objections to the way the Constitution was formed and ratified?
3. What solution does she propose?

CHAPTER 8

A NEW NATION FACING A REVOLUTIONARY WORLD, 1789 TO 1815

8.1. *GREENLEAF'S NEW YORK JOURNAL,* ANONYMOUS LETTERS REPORTING ON CROWD PROTESTS AGAINST THE JAY TREATY IN PHILADELPHIA (1795)

On July 8, 1795, the editor of *Greenleaf's New York Journal* printed two conflicting accounts of a protest against the Jay Treaty, the highly controversial treaty stabilizing relations between the United States and Great Britain. In the summer of 1795, the terms of the treaty were kept secret while the Senate decided whether to ratify it. But the secrecy did nothing to stop popular opposition. The Federalists and Democratic-Republicans battled not only over the treaty itself, but also over the specifics and meaning of protests like this one held by Philadelphia sailors.

Extract of a Letter from a respectable Citizen of Philadelphia, to his friend in this city. I must inform you of a circumstance which took place here on Saturday evening last. At eleven o'clock the ship-carpenters of Kensington, and a number of other citizens, about 500 armed with clubs, paraded the streets with a transparent painting of *Mr. Jay*; the figure in the attitude of presenting "THE TREATY" to an expecting, admiring Senate, with the left hand, and in the right, a pair of scales suspended—In the elevated scale, *"Virtue, Liberty and Independence,"* were inscribed in large capitals; in the preponderating one *"British Gold."* After passing through several streets, they returned again to Kensington, where the painting was *committed to the flames.* A small party of the Light-Horse attempted to disperse them, but without effect; they were driven from the field amidst a shower of stones, by which some were severely hurt, but no lives lost. I was an eyewitness to the whole proceeding, you may therefore rely on this account.

[Extract of another letter of the same date.]

The 4th of July passed over in quietness, whatever you may have heard to the contrary.

Source: Greenleaf's New York Journal, July 8, 1795.

On the fourth [of] July a number of ship carpenters from Kensington, and some of the Democratic Society, intended to burn Mr. Jay's effigy opposite the president's house. They were warned not to attempt it, and the militia officers, light horse, artillery, &c. waited for them in Market-street, till ten o'clock, but deterred them from their design, they came down Second to Market, from thence to Front, about one o'clock Sunday morning, as silent as a funeral procession, till they got above Vine street, and supposing themselves out of danger, when they gave three cheers. I mention this in case it becomes the subject of conversation. You may know how to speak of it.

Not ten persons in all the streets they passed knew any thing of it.

QUESTIONS

1. Judging from these two opposing accounts, what is possible to discern regarding the attitude of Philadelphia sailors and shipbuilders toward the Jay Treaty?
2. Which letter was likely written by a person with Democratic-Republican sympathies and which one by a person with Federalist sympathies?
3. Why would the New York newspaper publish these two conflicting accounts?

8.2. VISUAL DOCUMENT: ANONYMOUS CARTOONIST, THE *PROVIDENTIAL DETECTION* (c. 1797–1800)

In this, one of the earliest political cartoons published in the United States, an anonymous Federalist cartoonist uses a variety of images to paint a shocking picture of the Democratic-Republican front-runner in the 1800 election, Thomas Jefferson. The cartoon portrays him as a willing traitor to the United States who worships at the altar of revolutionary France—the "Altar of Gallic Despotism."

The eagle with the shield represents the United States as it swoops down to snatch the U.S. Constitution from a kneeling Jefferson before he can add the Constitution to the fire of French despotism. The French altar (which is supposed to recall similar altars to "Reason" that were used in high-profile radical revolutionary rituals in France) is surrounded by moneybags labeled "American Spoliations," "Plunder," "Sardinia," "Flanders," and with the names of other parts of Europe that France had invaded. A fire atop the altar is fed by radical writings—Democratic-Republican newspapers, including the *Aurora;* works by the English radical William Godwin; and French philosophical works by Rousseau and Voltaire. Falling from Jefferson's right hand is a copy of his famous letter to Philip Mazzei, an Italian diplomat and supporter of the French Revolution. The letter, which was published in a Paris newspaper in 1797, had criticized Federalists as monarchists and implied that George Washington was among them. The cartoon also contains religious imagery, showing the eye of Providence (God) looking down from the clouds and the Devil lurking behind the French altar.

Source: The Providential Detection. Courtesy American Antiquarian Society, Worcester, Massachusetts, USA/The Bridgeman Art Library.

QUESTIONS

1. How did the cartoonist communicate his belief that Jefferson was dangerous? Might any symbols or parts of the picture particularly move viewers?

2. Do you think the cartoon was effective? Could it have changed anyone's mind about the French Revolution? Did it probably appeal only to Federalists who already opposed Jefferson, or could it have had a broader appeal?

3. Why do you think the cartoonist decided to use a visual to make this argument about Jefferson, instead of writing a newspaper article or pamphlet?

8.3. JAMES BAYARD, EXCERPTS FROM A LETTER TO ALEXANDER HAMILTON DESCRIBING HIS DILEMMA IN THE DISPUTED PRESIDENTIAL ELECTION OF 1800 (JANUARY 7, 1801)

Delaware Congressman James Bayard was a loyal member of the Federalist Party. In this letter, he speculates to one of his party's leaders, Alexander Hamilton, about what might resolve the deadlocked presidential election and whether the Federalists in the House of Representatives would vote for Aaron Burr or Thomas Jefferson. When the ballots were cast in March, it was Bayard's vote that decided the election in favor of Jefferson.

I assure you, sir, there appears to be a strong inclination in a majority of the federal party to support Mr. Burr. The current has already acquired considerable force, and is manifestly increasing. The vote which the representation of a State enables me to give would decide the question in favor of Mr. Jefferson. At present I am by no means decided as to the object of preference. If the federal party should take up Mr. Burr, I ought certainly to be impressed with the most undoubting conviction before I separated myself from them. With respect to the personal qualities of the competitors, I should fear as much from the sincerity of Mr. Jefferson (if he is sincere), as from the want of probity in Mr. Burr. There would be really cause to fear that the government would not survive the course of moral and political experiments to which it would be subjected in the hands of Mr. Jefferson. But there is another view of the subject which gives me some inclination in favor of Burr. I consider the State ambition of Virginia as the source of present party. The faction who govern that State, aim to govern the United States. Virginia will never be satisfied but when this state of things exists. If Burr should be the President, they will not govern, and his acceptance of the office, which would disappoint their views, which depend upon Jefferson, would, I apprehend, immediately create a schism in the party which would soon rise into open opposition.

I cannot deny, however, that there are strong considerations, which give a preference to Mr. Jefferson. The subject admits of many doubtful views, and before I resolve on the part I shall take, I shall wait the approach of the crisis which may probably bring with it circumstances decisive of the event. The federal party meet on Friday, for the purpose of forming a resolution as to their line of conduct. I have not the least doubt of their agreeing to support Burr.

QUESTIONS

1. What are Bayard's objections to Jefferson and Burr?
2. Does this document offer evidence that the Federalists had become a well-organized political party by 1801?

Source: Allen Johnson, ed., Readings in American Constitutional History, 1776–1876 (New York: Houghton Mifflin Company, 1913), 214–15.

8.4. JAMES MATHER AND WILLIAM CLAIBORNE, EXCERPTS FROM LETTERS REGARDING CARIBBEAN MIGRANTS IN NEW ORLEANS (1809)

On July 18, 1809, James Mather, the mayor of New Orleans, wrote to Louisiana's territorial governor, William Claiborne, about refugees from the Haitian revolution who had come to New Orleans from Cuba. The emigrants, a mix of whites, free people of color, and slaves, presented a challenge to the city. Congress eventually passed a special exemption to the prohibition on the international importation of slaves to allow these slaves to be brought into the United States from Cuba.

In answer to your much esteemed [letter] of yesterday, I beg leave to enclose here in for the information of your Excellency, a general statement of the People brought here from the Island of Cuba by thirty four vessels. . . . It is hardly possible to form as yet a Judgement on the general character of the different classes.—It may however be inferred from their conduct since they have lived among us, as also from various other circumstances.

1stly In what regards the Blacks, they are trained up to the habits of strict discipline, and consist wholly of Africans bought up from guineamen in the island of Cuba, or of faithful slaves who have fled with their masters from St. Domingo as early as the year 1803.

2dly A few characters among the free People of Color have been represented to me as dangerous for the peace of this Territory; I must however own your Excellency that in every other Territory but this, the most part of them would not, I think, be viewed under the same light if due attention should be paid to the effects of the difference of language, and if it should be considered that these very men possess property, and have useful trades to live upon[1]. . . . In the mean time there has not been one single complaint that I know of; against any of them concerning their conduct since their coming to this place.

3rdly The white persons, consisting chiefly of Planters, and merchants of St. Domingo who took refuge on the shores of Cuba about six years ago, appear to be an active, industrious People. . . . They have suffered a great deal from the want of Provisions both at sea, and in the River.—Several of them have died, and many are now yet a prey to diseases originating, as it appears, from the use of unwholesome food and from the foul air they have breathed, while heaped up together with their slaves, in the holds of small vessels during their passage from Cuba. . . .

I know of no provision established by our Laws, to prevent free white persons who have means for their living, to come and settle in the United States. . . .

[On November 5, 1809, William Claiborne wrote to Secretary of State Robert Smith to express his suspicion and concern about the refugees from Haiti who had come into New Orleans through Cuba and Jamaica.]

At all times, the *utmost vigilance* on the part of the officers of the Government in this Territory, is essential, but it is particularly so at the present period, when foreigners and *Strangers* are daily arriving among us; of *whom*, many are of doubtful character and desperate fortunes, and may (probably) become willing instruments in the hands of those unprincipled, intriguing

---

Source: Dunbar Rowland, ed., *Official Letter Books of W. C. C. Claiborne, 1801–1816*, reprinted. (New York: AMS Press, 1976), 4:387–88, 422–23; 5: 1–2.

1. The free people of color were required to post bond and leave the territory within a set amount of time.

individuals, who would wish to disturb the *peace, and Union* of the American States. . . .

You are already acquainted with the difficulty and anxiety which the Emigrants from Cuba occasioned me;—I anticipate like difficulties with the French Emigrants from Sto. Domingo and Jamaica, who I suspect will repair hither with their slaves.

[Just days later, on November 12, 1809, Claiborne again wrote to Secretary Smith about refugees from Haiti who were entering New Orleans from Cuba and Jamaica and bringing slaves with them. He feared that the city could not handle the influx of people, and that the international slave trade would be reopened, despite its being outlawed by Congress the previous year.]

Two or three vessels from the City of Sto. Domingo via Jamaica have recently arrived in the Mississippi, with passengers and some slaves on board and others are expected.—

Already New Orleans and its vicinity are crowded with the unfortunate refugees from Cuba, and if the French of St. Domingo, Jamaica (& perhaps Guadeloupe, for I am told it is about to [be] attacked) should also seek an asylum here, I shall deem it alike unfortunate for them and for us;—for independent political considerations, this society will be totally unable to furnish conveniences for so numerous and sudden an emigration, or to supply the wants of the poor and distressed. I am particularly desirous to discourage the Emigrants from bringing slaves with them.—Motives of humanity induce me to permit the Refugees from Cuba to land their slaves, but this indulgence cannot be extended much farther, for already Sir, it is represented to me, that Negro's purchased from the Jails of Jamaica, have been smuggled into the Territory, and I suspect if it was understood, that Negro's brought by the French of St. Domingo were permitted to be landed, that a Negro trade hither would be immediately commenced.— These considerations Sir, induced me to write the Letters to our Consuls at Havanah and Jamaica, and I hope the same will be approved by the President.—

QUESTIONS

1. What problems do the mayor and the governor anticipate that the new arrivals from the Caribbean will bring with them to New Orleans?
2. Why did government officials accept these refugees if they were so troublesome?
3. What evidence does this document present about the ways that Caribbean immigrants confused and challenged Americans' racial attitudes?

8.5. VISUAL DOCUMENT: JOHN WESLEY JARVIS, PORTRAIT OF CAPTAIN SAMUEL CHESTER REID (1815)

John Wesley Jarvis painted this portrait of Captain Samuel Chester Reid in 1815 just after the War of 1812. During the war, Reid captained a privateer, the *General Armstrong*, that conducted raids in the Azores Islands, about halfway between Portugal and the United States. In 1814, he engaged British naval forces bound for Jamaica and New Orleans, and Andrew Jackson claimed that Reid's actions slowed British naval reinforcements down sufficiently to aid his triumphal defense of New Orleans. Reid's naval heroism was publicly applauded and became the subject of popular engravings, some of which may have used this portrait as a source. In 1817, Reid designed the present pattern of the U.S. flag with thirteen stripes and one star for each state, and the flag in the background of this portrait is a close forerunner of his stars and stripes design.

Source: John Wesley Jarvis, "Captain Samuel Chester Reid," 1815, Minneapolis Institute of Arts.

QUESTIONS

1. What visual aspects of this portrait of Reid indicate that he is a heroic figure?
2. What is the impression of naval warfare given by this portrait?

3. Can you tell anything about American national identity by examining this portrait, or is it better understood just as a picture of one, heroic man?

CHAPTER 9

AMERICAN PEOPLES ON THE MOVE, 1789 TO 1824

9.1. JOURNAL OF BENJAMIN CARPENTER, *REFLECTIONS ON THE INDIA TRADE* (1790)

Benjamin Carpenter captained his merchant ship, the *Ruby*, from Boston in 1789 hoping to trade at Port Louis in the Mauritius Islands, but when he arrived there, he found the French port in an upheaval caused by the French Revolution. He sailed to Ceylon (Sri Lanka) instead and then to India to continue trading first in Madras and then in Calcutta. Here, he comments in his ship journal about U.S. trade prospects in India.

On your arrival at Calcutta you will proceed as at Madras—the manner and customs are the same with this difference only—the inhabitants are more sociable and friendly. You will find them ready to assist you in everything. They are very liberal and deal on honorable terms. On my arrival at Bengal I was an utter stranger to every person there—and notwithstanding I was destitute of even a line of recommendation, I found the greatest hospitality and very soon became acquainted with the principal merchants there.

The produce and manufactories of Bengal are every way suited for the American market, but as the trade to this country is a very recent affair, they have not those goods on hand which we are most in want of. For this reason our ships are obliged to wait three

or four months for a cargo. This inconvenience is easily remedied by a previous order. You may then be sure to have your goods in readiness on your arrival, and then your detention may not be more than three weeks or a month. . . .

A voyage from America may be performed in fourteen months—and a person well acquainted with a suitable cargo will seldom fail to make a good voyage. Their sugar and niter will ballast your ship, you can fill her with dry goods. The sugar is of a superior quality to West India sugar and is sold at six rupees per maund of eighty-two pounds English. The country abounds with a great variety of drugs of the first qualities. . . . They are sold astonishingly cheap, and if care is taken in choosing them they will turn to very good account in

Source: Benjamin Carpenter, "From the Journal of the *Ruby*, 1789–1790," in *Yankee India: American Commercial and Cultural Encounters with India in the Age of Sail, 1784–1860*, ed. Susan S. Bean, 61–63 (Salem, MA: Peabody Essex Museum, 2001).

Europe. There is many articles in Bengal which would answer well in America that we are not yet acquainted with. There are also many things [that are] the produce of America that would net good profit and would be a sure remittance in India. . . .

America abounds with furs of different kinds, any quantity of the various species would very readily sell in Bengal at 100 percent profit. They purchase them to send to China, which is by far the best remittance they can make. It is a little surprising that [given] the number of ships we have sent to China that none of them should think of furs. They are certainly the best article they can carry. . . .

3000 barrels of whale oil would readily sell in Calcutta for 20 Rupees on the barrel which is double the price it sells at in America. . . .

After duly considering the advantage arising from this trade, there is no one can venture to affirm that the commerce with India is prejudicial to America. . . .

Having contracted for a quantity of chintz to be manufactured at Chandernagore (a French factory about 30 miles from Calcutta). In order to choose patterns and expedite matters, I this morning hired a buggerow and made an excursion up the river. . . .

The navigation to Chandernagore is perfectly safe and there is a sufficient depth of water for a vessel of 1,000 tons to anchor within a cable's length of the shore. If we can conquer the silly jealousies subsisting between the American merchants and persuade them to unite their property to establish a factory here, I am fully persuaded they would realize forty percent per annum on their stock. This is certainly a far greater profit than they can gain on their Europe, West India or any other trade whatever.

QUESTIONS

1. What kinds of goods does this document show were involved in the U.S.–India trade?
2. Why would this description make the India trade sound attractive to prospective ship captains?
3. How did economics influence Carpenter's view of India?

9.2. ELI WHITNEY AND THOMAS JEFFERSON, LETTERS ON THE PATENTING OF THE COTTON GIN (1793)

On June 20, 1793, Eli Whitney wrote to Secretary of State Thomas Jefferson requesting a patent for the cotton gin that he had recently invented. Congress empowered the secretary of state to grant a patent to anyone who submitted a description of an invention, drawings, a model, and a fee. Whitney's letter and Jefferson's reply of November 16, 1793 are reproduced below.

That having invented a Machine for the Purpose of ginning Cotton, he is desirous of obtaining an exclusive Property in the same. Concerning which invention, your Petitioner alledges as follows (viz) first. That it is entirely new and constructed in a different manner and upon different principles from any, other Cotton Gin or Machine heretofore known or used for that purpose. 2d. That with this Ginn, if turned with horses or by water, two persons will clean as much cotton in one Day, as a Hundred persons could cleane

Sources: John Catanzariti, ed., *The Papers of Thomas Jefferson*, vol. 26 (Princeton, N.J.: Princeton University Press, 1995); Eli Whitney Papers, Yale University Library.

in the same time with the gins now in common use. 3d. That the Cotton which is cleansed in his Ginn contains fewer broken seeds and impurities, and is said to be more valuable than Cotton, which is cleaned in the usual way. Your Petitioner, therefore Prays your Honor to Grant him the said Whitney, a Patent for the said Invention or Improvement. . . .

[November 16, 1793]

Your favor of October 18, including a drawing [of] your cotton gin, was received. . . . The only requisite of the law now uncomplied with is the forwarding of a model, which being received your patent may be made out & delivered to your order immediately. As the state of Virginia, of which I am, carries on household manufactures of cotton to a great extent, as I also do myself, and one of our great embarrassments in the cleaning the cotton of the seed, I feel a considerable interest in the success of your invention, for family use. Permit me therefore to ask information from you on these points, has the machine been thoroughly tried in the ginning of cotton, or is it as yet but a machine of theory? What quantity of cotton has it cleaned on an average of several days, & worked by hand, & by how many hands? What will be the cost of one of these made to be worked by hand? Favorable answers to these questions would induce me to engage one of them to be forwarded to Richmond for me.

QUESTIONS

1. What claims for improvement in cotton gin design does Whitney make?
2. What aspects of the new gin most interest Jefferson?
3. Why was it important for Eli Whitney to apply for a federal patent for his invention? What did it gain him?

9.3. SUSANNAH ROWSON, PREFACE TO *CHARLOTTE TEMPLE* (1794)

Novelist Susannah Rowson explained the purpose of her novel *Charlotte Temple* in the preface to the Philadelphia edition of the book. She argued that her novel should not be seen as dangerous for young women, as many novels were perceived to be at the turn of the nineteenth century. The publisher of this edition of the work, Matthew Carey, also preceded the novel with this review from a contemporary magazine.

It may be a Tale of Truth, for it is not unnatural, and it is a tale of real distress—Charlotte, by the artifice of a teacher . . . is enticed from her governess, and accompanies a young officer to America.—The marriage ceremony, if not forgotten, is postponed, and Charlotte dies a martyr to the inconstancy of her lover and treachery of his friend.—The situations are artless and affecting—the descriptions natural and pathetic; we should feel for Charlotte, if such a person ever existed, who, for one error, scarcely, perhaps, deserved so severe a punishment. If it is a fiction, poetic justice is not, we think, properly distributed.

Source: Susannah Rowson, *Charlotte: A Tale of Truth*, vol. 1, 2nd ed. (Philadelphia: Matthew Carey, 1794).

For the perusal of the young and thoughtless of the fair sex, this Tale of Truth is designed; and I could wish my fair readers to consider it as not merely the effusion of Fancy, but as a reality. The circumstances on which I have founded this novel were related to me some little time since by an old lady who had personally known Charlotte, though she concealed the real names of the characters, and likewise the place where the unfortunate scenes were acted: yet as it was impossible to offer a relation to the public in such an imperfect state, I have thrown over the whole a slight veil of fiction, and substituted names and places according to my own fancy. The principal characters in this little tale are now consigned to the silent tomb: it can therefore hurt the feelings of no one; and may, I flatter myself, be of service to some who are so unfortunate as to have neither friends to advise, or understanding to direct them, through the various and unexpected evils that attend a young and unprotected woman in her first entrance into life.

While the tear of compassion still trembled in my eye for the fate of the unhappy Charlotte, I may have children of my own, said I, to whom this recital may be of use, and if to your own children, said Benevolence, why not to the many daughters of Misfortune who, deprived of natural friends, or spoilt by a mistaken education, are thrown on an unfeeling world without the least power to defend themselves from the snares not only of the other sex, but from the more dangerous arts of the profligate of their own.

Sensible as I am that a novel writer, at a time when such a variety of works are ushered into the world under that name, stands but a poor chance for fame in the annals of literature, but conscious that I wrote with a mind anxious for the happiness of that sex whose morals and conduct have so powerful an influence on mankind in general; and convinced that I have not wrote a line that conveys a wrong idea to the head or a corrupt wish to the heart, I shall rest satisfied in the purity of my own intentions, and if I merit not applause, I feel that I dread not censure.

If the following tale should save one hapless fair one from the errors which ruined poor Charlotte, or rescue from impending misery the heart of one anxious parent, I shall feel a much higher gratification in reflecting on this trifling performance, than could possibly result from the applause which might attend the most elegant finished piece of literature whose tendency might deprave the heart or mislead the understanding.

QUESTIONS

1. How does Rowson argue that her novel can teach good morals to young women?
2. What does this document indicate about public opinion in the 1790s on the nature of women?
3. After reading the novel's introduction, why do you think *Charlotte Temple* became so popular among readers, especially women?

9.4. VISUAL DOCUMENT: *TODDY JUG WITH PORTRAIT OF GEORGE WASHINGTON* (c. 1800–1820)

This porcelain jug, made to serve hot alcoholic beverages, belonged to Edward Tilghman, a Philadelphia lawyer. Tilghman's uncle, Benjamin Chew Wilcocks, ordered the jug from China, where it was manufactured and hand decorated. The portrait on the jug copies an engraving by David Edwin of a Gilbert Stuart portrait of Washington.

QUESTIONS

1. Why would Americans want to have pictures of George Washington on household objects like this one?

2. What does this object tell us about the relationship between the United States and China at the beginning of the nineteenth century?

Source: "Toddy jug with portrait of George Washington [Chinese for the American market] (34.74a.b)". In *Heilbrunn Timeline of Art History* (New York: The Metropolitan Museum of Art, 2000). http://www.metmuseum.org/toah/works-of-art/34.74a.b (May 2009).

CHAPTER 10

MARKET REVOLUTIONS AND THE RISE OF DEMOCRACY, 1789 TO 1832

10.1. WILLIAM SAMPSON, EXCERPTS FROM *PEOPLE V. MELVIN* IN DEFENSE OF THE NEW YORK JOURNEYMEN SHOEMAKERS (1809)

Attorney William Sampson, a Jacobin revolutionary émigré from France, defended New York's journeymen shoemakers when they were prosecuted in 1809 for illegally colluding to go on strike and win a wage increase. In this case, *People v. Melvin*, Sampson made an eloquent speech that argued that the journeymen deserved a fair chance in the changing market economy.

Shall all others, except only the industrious mechanic, be allowed to meet and plot; merchants to determine their prices current, or settle the markets, politicians to electioneer, sportsmen for horseracing and games, ladies and gentlemen for balls, parties and bouquets; and yet those poor men be indicted for combining against starvation? I ask again, is this repugnant to the rights of man? If it be, is it not repugnant to our constitution? If it be repugnant to our constitution, is it law? And if it is not law, shall we be put to answer to it?

If it be said, they have wages enough, or too much already, I do not think any man a good witness to that point but one who has himself laboured. If either of the gentlemen opposed to us will take his station in the garret or cellar of one of these industrious men, get a leather apron and a strap, a last, a lap-stone and a hammer, and peg and stitch from five in the morning till eight in the evening, and feed and educate his family with what he so earns, then if he will come into court, and say upon his corporal oath that he was, during that probation too much pampered or indulged, I will consider whether these men may not be extortioners. . . .

Like most other societies of the same nature, the journeymen shoemakers' society is a charitable institution.

Source: John R. Commons, Ulrich B. Phillips, Eugene A. Gilmore, Helen L. Sumner, and John B. Andrews, eds., *Documentary History of American Industrial Society*, vol. 3 (Cleveland, Ohio: Arthur H. Clark Company, 1910), 279–80, 299–300.

They raise a fund, which is sacred to the use of their helpless or unfortunate members, and to the relief of the widows and orphans of their departed brethren. . . . And to induce every one to join the society, while by his labour he may make something to spare for their fund, they refuse to work with any one who is so wanting in charity as not to join them. . . . Who will say that an association of this nature is illegal? . . . The masters were in the habit of crowding their shops with more apprentices than they could instruct. Two was thought as many as one man could do justice by. The journeymen shoemakers therefore determined to set their faces against the rapacity of the masters, and refused to work for those who were so unjust as to delude with the promise of instruction which it was impossible they could give. . . .

It is to be observed, that neither of these counts charge that the design of the defendants was to raise their wages. And though it should be admitted that a conspiracy to raise their wages would subject the defendants to an indictment, yet I doubt if any authority can be found to support an indictment for charges like these.

QUESTIONS

1. What is the basis for Sampson's defense of the journeymen shoemakers?
2. Does this document show evidence that the journeymen were developing a sense of belonging to a working class that was separate from the master craftsmen for whom they worked?
3. How does Sampson's insistence on the "rights of man" relate to the ideas of the American Revolution and the French Revolution?

10.2. BASIL HALL, EXCERPTS FROM *TRAVELS IN NORTH AMERICA IN THE YEARS 1827 AND 1828* (1829)

In 1829, Basil Hall, a British naval officer from a Scottish aristocratic family, published a book recounting his travels in North America in the previous two years. In this selection, Hall describes parts of upstate New York and western Massachusetts, where he met people with many ideas about how to improve American transportation and trade.

On the 3d of October, 1827, we left Stockbridge, and proceeded across the country to Northampton, another of those beautiful New England villages, which it is impossible to overpraise. Our road was conducted through ravines, over mountain passes, and occasionally along the very summit of ridges, from whence we commanded a view of sufficient beauty to redeem, in the course of one morning, all the flatness and insipidity of our previous journey. The greater part, indeed, of the country which we had yet seen—always, of course, excepting the beautiful Lake George, and delightful Hudson—consisted either of ploughed fields, or impenetrable forests, or it was spotted over with new villages, as raw and unpicturesque as if

Source: Basil Hall, *Travels in North America in the Years 1827 and 1828*, vol. 2 (Edinburgh: Cadell and Co., 1829), 93–94, 100–101.

they had just stepped out of a saw-pit. The towns of Massachusetts, on the contrary, were embellished with ornamental trees and flower gardens, while the larger features of the landscape owed their interest to the more vigorous accompaniments of rocks, mountains, waterfalls, and all the varied lights and shades of Alpine scenery.

In the course of this agreeable day's journey, we traversed a considerable portion of the route over which it has been seriously proposed, I was assured, to carry a rail-road between the cities of Boston and Albany. No single State, still less any Section of the Union, it seems, likes to be outdone by any other State; and this feeling of rivalry, stimulated by the success of the great Erie Canal—is an undertaking highly favoured by nature—has, I supposed suggested the visionary project in question. In answer to the appeals frequently made to my admiration of this scheme, I was compelled to admit, that there was much boldness in the conception; but I took the liberty of adding, that I conceived the boldness lay in the conception alone; for, if it were executed, its character would be changed into madness.

Albany and Boston lie nearly east and west of each other; while much of the intermediate space is so completely ribbed over by a series of high ridges running north and south, that the rail-way in question would have to pass along a sort of gigantic corduroy road, over a country altogether unsuited for such an undertaking. Besides which, several navigable rivers, and more than one canal, lying along the intermediate valleys, connect the interior with the sea, and thus afford far readier means of exporting or importing goods to or from New York, Albany, or Boston, than any railway can ever furnish.

The same reasoning might be applied to a hundred other projects in the United States, many of them not less impracticable, but which, although existing only on paper, are, nevertheless assumed completed, and cast into the balance of American greatness, till the imaginary scale, loaded with anticipated magnificence, makes the Old World kick the beam, to the great satisfaction of the inhabitants of this country, and the admiration of distant lands, who know nothing of the matter. . . .

At Worcester I met a remarkably intelligent person, with whom I fell into conversation on the subject of manufactures, and the measure which was then in agitation, and has since been carried, of protecting, as it is called, the domestic industry of that country by a new Tariff, or higher scale of duties on imported goods.

He contended that the manufactures of New England in particular, but also those of other parts of the Union, had grown up during the late war, when foreign goods were excluded, and had been enabled to flourish, more or less, ever since, in consequence of the protecting duties laid on foreign articles by the General Government.

QUESTIONS

1. Hall claims that Europeans exaggerate the greatness of American transportation and manufacturing, yet he seems impressed himself. Why?
2. How do Hall's observations offer evidence both of states working together to implement internal improvements and of jealousies between states?
3. What is the relationship between nature and technological improvement in Hall's description of the United States?

10.3. VISUAL DOCUMENT: *PAPER ELECTION TICKET FOR MARYLAND GENERAL ASSEMBLY (1828)*

This paper election ticket is a piece of material culture, a physical object, that can allow us to understand what it was like to take part in the new democratic politics of the 1820s. The ticket was printed in Baltimore in 1828 to promote the Democratic candidacy of John Van Laer McMahon and George H. Steuart for the Maryland legislature. One of the tools the new Democratic party electioneering that was taking place in 1828 was the distribution of paper ballots like this one—which associated the local candidates with presidential candidate Andrew Jackson and with past Democratic-Republican president Thomas Jefferson. While campaigning and voting had both gained new importance among white men in 1828, the process was not identical to politics in the 21st century. Elections were conducted in public, and secret ballots did not begin to be required in the United States until after 1888. Voters often accepted election tickets like this one from party bosses, labor unions, and other campaign workers. States did not print official ballots, and voters could cast their votes using highly partisan ballots like this one.

Source: "Jackson Ticket," 1828. Library of Congress Rare Books and Special Collections Division.

QUESTIONS

1. How does the ballot use text and images to link the local candidates to Jackson and Jefferson? Why would that appeal to many voters?
2. Other Democratic tickets printed for the same 1828 election featured mottos like "Jackson Ticket: Agriculture, Commerce, and Manufactures" and "Jackson Ticket: Firm united let us be, Rallying round our Hickory tree." Which ticket do you think would appeal to which voters the most?
3. Would seeing and touching a physical object like this election ticket make a voter a better participant in the democratic election, or did party control of the ballot decrease individual choice?

10.4. EDITOR OF *THE EASTERN ARGUS*, EXCERPTS FROM COVERAGE OF FOURTH OF JULY CELEBRATIONS IN PORTLAND, MAINE (JULY 9, 1830)

The editor of *The Eastern Argus*, the Democratic-Republican newspaper in Portland, Maine, reported on Fourth of July celebrations that took place in that city in 1830 in partisan terms. Newspapers in the 1830s were an important organ of political party development and organization.

The Anniversary of American Independence was celebrated on Monday last, by the Republicans of Portland, in a style never equaled upon a like occasion in this State.

The illiberal and disingenuous course pursued in advance of the day, by the mangers of what has been called the *Town Celebration*, aroused a proper sense of self respect in Republicans, who resolved spontaneously, as it were, not to submit to the indignity of it. . . . Preparations were consequently made for a celebration among themselves, in self defence. . . .

The inside was tastefully decorated throughout with green boughs, evergreen and roses, historical paintings and engravings. Over the arched entrance from the street, stood erect, during the day, a beautiful, full grown, living American Eagle, whose fine appearance excited the admiration of thousands. Upon the face of the arch beneath, was inscribed the republican motto—VOX POPULI! On the inner side surrounded by other appropriate decorations, were two full rigged vessels in miniature suspended from the arch, and on the sides of the walk beneath were the portraits of Washington, Jefferson, and Jackson, as if to preside over and cheer the festivities of the occasion. . . .

At noon a procession was formed. . . . We believe we expose ourselves to the contradiction of no candid and disinterested man, in saying that this procession was decidedly the most numerous ever witnessed in this town, on any previous occasion. In passing through Middle Street the procession for the "town celebration" was met with, and the two parties passed each other under a military salute. . . .

After the services at the Meeting-house were concluded, the procession re-organized and passed up Federal Street . . . to the bower, where five hundred and

Source: *The Eastern Argus*, July 9, 1830.

sixty eight persons partook of a dinner, provided by Mr. ATWOOD. . . .

[Toasts were then given.]

By Gen. J. W. Smith, Vice President, *Those sacred Democratic principles of the party*, which in 1801 called forth the immortal Jefferson, and in 1829, the hero and illustrious patriot Jackson, to preside over this great and happy republic. . . .

By Doct. B. H. Mace. V. P. *The Democracy of New Hampshire*—Founded on a rock—Firm as the *Hills*, its pillars stand unmoved. . . .

By Mr. Daniel Robinson, V. P. *Andrew Jackson, President of the United States*—May he live to a good old age, for the benefit of the rising generation. . . .

By Hon. Wm. Chadwick. *The Hon'ble John Anderson, our Representative in Congress*—His untiring industry and successful exertions in behalf of our commercial interests, justly entitle him to the warmest gratitude of his constituents. . . .

By Hon. Luther Fitch. *The Fourth of July*—The anniversary of American Independence—the time to revert to the essential principles of the republic—to impress them upon the mind and the heart, that they may never be forgotten or abandoned.

QUESTIONS

1. How did this celebration seek to link Portland's Democratic Republicans to the glory of America's past?

2. What were the partisan elements of the celebration? Which parts seemed to be purely patriotic?

3. How would you compare the toasts at this Fourth of July celebration to current-day political campaigning?

10.5. ANDREW JACKSON, VETO OF THE BANK OF THE UNITED STATES (JULY 10, 1832)

When Andrew Jackson vetoed the reauthorization of the charter of the Second Bank of the United States in July 1832, he issued this message to explain his actions. Jackson later backed up his veto by withdrawing all federal funds from the bank and eventually triumphed in his political war with Nicholas Biddle, the bank's president.

A bank of the United States is in many respects convenient for the Government and useful to the people. . . . I sincerely regret that in the act before me I can perceive none of those modifications of the bank charter which are necessary, in my opinion, to make it compatible with justice, with sound policy, or with the Constitution of our country. . . .

Every monopoly and all exclusive privileges are granted at the expense of the public, which ought to receive a fair equivalent. The many millions which this act proposes to bestow on the stockholders of the existing bank must come directly or indirectly out of the earnings of the American people. . . .

It is to be regretted that the rich and powerful too often bend the acts of government to their selfish purposes. Distinctions in society will always exist under every just government. Equality of talents, of education, or of wealth can not be produced by human institutions. In the full enjoyment of the gifts of Heaven and the fruits of superior industry, economy, and virtue,

Source: Francis Newton, ed., *The Statesmanship of Andrew Jackson as Told in His Writings and Speeches* (New York: Tandy-Thomas Company, 1909), 155–76.

every man is equally entitled to protection by law; but when the laws undertake to add to these natural and just advantages artificial distinctions, to grant titles, gratuities, and exclusive privileges, to make the rich richer and the potent more powerful, the humble members of society—the farmers, mechanics, and laborers—who have neither the time nor the means of securing like favors to themselves, have a right to complain of the injustice of Government. There are no necessary evils in government. Its evils exist only in its abuses. . . .

Nor is our Government to be maintained or our Union preserved by invasions of the rights and powers of the several States. In thus attempting to make our General Government strong we make it weak. Its true strength consists in leaving individuals and States as much as possible to themselves—in making itself felt, not in its power, but in its beneficence; not in its control, but in its protection; not in binding the States more closely to the center, but leaving each to move unobstructed in its proper orbit. . . .

I have now done my duty to my country. If sustained by my fellow-citizens, I shall be grateful and happy; if not, I shall find in the motives which impel me ample grounds for contentment and peace. In the difficulties which surround us and the dangers which threaten our institutions there is cause for neither dismay or alarm. For relief and deliverance let us firmly rely on that kind of Providence which I am sure watches with peculiar care over the destinies of our Republic, and on the intelligence and wisdom of our countrymen.

QUESTIONS

1. What were Jackson's main objections to the bank charter?
2. What can you tell about Jackson's idea of democracy based upon his objections to the bank?
3. What relationship does Jackson describe between the national government and the states?

CHAPTER 11

NEW BOUNDARIES, NEW ROLES, 1820 TO 1856

11.1. VISUAL DOCUMENT: FAN WITH VIEW OF FOREIGN FACTORIES AT CANTON (1790–1800)

In the late 18th century, European traders desperately tried to gain access to Chinese markets. The Chinese restricted their trading "factories" (or warehouses) to a confined section of Canton. This fan is one of many small consumer goods that would have been carried back to the United States.

Source: The Granger Collection, NYC. All rights reserved.

QUESTIONS

1. What would American consumers have made of this object?
2. What does the array of European flags and facilities suggest about Chinese authority?
3. Why is the fence around the trading facility only present on the seaward side?

11.2. CHEROKEE WOMEN, "PETITION" (JUNE 30, 1818)

During the early nineteenth century, the United States pressured the Cherokee Nation to sell their lands and move west. At different times, some Cherokee leaders agreed to terms but these men never represented a majority of the Cherokee community. Each transaction created debate and acrimony among Cherokees. The petition below is from the Cherokee Women's Council. While men were usually the dominant political figures, these women represented the matrilineal clans who, according to Cherokee belief, owned the Cherokee homeland. Thus, when it came to matters of land, women spoke with authority.

Beloved Children,

We have called a meeting among ourselves to consult on the different points now before the council, relating to our national affairs. We have heard with painful feelings that the bounds of the land we now possess are to be drawn into very narrow limits. The land was given to us by the Great Spirit above as our common right, to raise our children upon, & to make support for our rising generations. We therefore humbly petition our beloved children, the head men & warriors, to hold out to the last in support of our common rights, as the Cherokee nation have been the first settlers of this land; we therefore claim the right of the soil.

We well remember that our country was formerly very extensive, but by repeated sales it has become circumscribed to the very narrow limits we have at present. Our Father the President advised us to become farmers, to manufacture our own clothes, & to have our children instructed. To this advice we have attended in every thing as far as we were able. Now the thought of being compelled to remove the other side of the Mississippi is dreadful to us, because it appears to us that we, by this removal, shall be brought to a savage state again, for we have, by the endeavor of our Father the President, become too much enlightened to throw aside the privileges of a civilized life.

We therefore unanimously join in our meeting to hold our country in common as hitherto. Some of our children have become Christians. We have missionary schools among us. We have heard the gospel in our nation. We have become civilized & enlightened, & are in hopes that in a few years our nation will be prepared for instruction in other branches of sciences & arts, which are both useful & necessary in civilized society.

Source: Theda Purdue and Michael D. Green, *The Cherokee Removal: A Brief History with Sources* (Boston: Bedford-St. Martin's, 2005), p.132–33.

There are some white men among us who have been raised in this country from their youth, are connected with us by marriage, & have considerable families, who are very active in encouraging the emigration of our nation. These ought to be our truest friends but prove our worst enemies. They seem to be only concerned how to increase their riches, but do not care what becomes of our Nation, nor even of their own wives and children.

QUESTIONS

1. On what grounds do the petitioners oppose the emigration of Cherokee to Indian Territory?
2. How do the petitioners portray the Cherokee nation and its relations with the United States and with Anglo Americans?
3. What conclusions can we draw from this source about the role of women in Cherokee politics?

11.3. *THE PHALANX*, EXCERPTS FROM "THE STRIKE FOR WAGES" (NOVEMBER 4, 1843) AND "THE TEN HOUR SYSTEM" (MAY 18, 1844)

In the 1820s and 1830s, workers began going on strike to gain higher wages. When these efforts failed, labor leaders began advocating policy changes to protect laboring people. The *Phalanx* was one of many small workers' newspapers that flourished in northeastern cities.

THE STRIKE FOR WAGES

There has been a very general "turn-out" in all the Atlantic cities among the working classes. In every trade almost there has been a strike for higher wages, and generally the demands of the workmen have been complied with by the "masters." The reaction in the commercial world has stimulated business a little, which has increased slightly the demand for labor, and as the population of this country has not yet become dense and excessive, the working classes by the subversive means of counter-coalitions to those which exist under our present false system of Industry and Commerce—leagues of wealth and industrial monopoly—are enabled to obtain a small advance of wages. But how trifling and pitiful an amount of benefit, after all, they receive, by such means, even when and for the time they do succeed; and how miserably inadequate to meet their wants and satisfy their rights, are such beggarly additions to their wages. Will not the working classes, the intelligent producers of this country, see what a miserable shift and expedient to better their condition is a "strike for wages?" Will they not see how uncertain the tenure by which they hold the little advantage they gain by it? Will they not see how degrading the position which forces them to appeal to and beg concessions of employers? Will they not see this and a thousand other evils connected with a false system of industry, and learn that the only remedy is a union among themselves to produce for themselves, to associate, and combine, and owning the land on which they live and the tools and machinery with which they work, enjoy the products of their own labor? We hope so, and then all such "civilized" false association, will be unnecessary. . . .

Source: John R. Commons, Ulrich B. Phillips, Eugene A. Gilmore, Helen L. Sumner, and John B. Andrews, eds., *A Documentary History of American Industrial Society*, vol. 7 (Cleveland, Ohio: Arthur Clark, 1910), 231–33.

THE TEN HOUR SYSTEM

The agitation of the subject of a reduction of the time of labor in factories is not, however, confined to England; in this country, the evils of the factory system in the exaction of an undue portion of the time of the laborer—twelve, fourteen, and even sixteen and eighteen hours out of the twenty-four, and in the excessive toil imposed on young children, have been severely felt. In a general way the subject has occupied the attention of politicians, from time to time, as elections were pending, and a vast deal of demagogism has been expended on it; but latterly it has been specially considered by the Legislature of Pennsylvania, and now in New England great feeling is manifested towards it in some of the manufacturing towns. An association of mechanics has been formed at Fall River, Massachusetts, for the special purpose of reducing the duration of labor to ten hours per day, and to effect this object, has started a spirited little sheet called the *Mechanic*. We wish, however, that we could impress upon our countrymen the degrading littleness and insufficiency of this attempt at a compromise of their rights, for it is neither more nor less than a demeaning compromise and dastardly sacrifice of their rights, for them to make terms which only modifies the condition but does not change the terms of dependence on masters.

In wretched England, where the laborer is indeed a poor, degraded, helpless being, it is well that any amelioration can be obtained; but here, where the laboring classes are intelligent and generally possess the ability to do full justice to themselves, it does appear to us to be excessively weak and trifling, if not disgraceful, for them to talk about a reform which at the most can relieve them temporarily of a few hours' oppressive toil—can convert them from twelve and fourteen to ten hour slaves—but cannot elevate them to the dignity of true independence! What a farce is boasted American freedom, if free-men are reduced to such beggarly shifts! Do they not see that they exhibit the badge of slavery in the very effort to mitigate its oppression? Free-men would not talk about terms which involve only a question of time of subjection to the authority and will of another—they would consult and act for their own good in all things without let or hindrance!

QUESTIONS

1. Why does the *Phalanx* argue against workers using strikes as a means of protest?
2. What is the newspaper's attitude toward a ten-hour workday?
3. What kind of solution does the paper recommend?

11.4. JOSÉ ENRIQUE DE LA PEÑA, EXCERPT FROM *WITH SANTA ANNA IN TEXAS: A PERSONAL NARRATIVE OF THE REVOLUTION* (1836)

In 1835, an independence movement composed of Spanish—and English—speaking residents of Mexico's northernmost state of Coahuila erupted. This movement attracted Americans, who fought on behalf of the rebels. Mexican forces, led by Antonio Lopez de Santa Anna, attacked the rebels, most famously at the Alamo, a former mission in San Antonio. De la Peña was a soldier with Santa Anna's army in the attack at the Alamo, in which all the defenders were killed.

Source: "José Enrique de la Peña, 1836," Published as *With Santa Anna In Texas: A Personal Narrative of the Revolution by José Enrique de la Peña*, ed. Carmen Perry (College Station: Texas A&M Press, 1975), 38–57.

On the 17th of February the commander in chief had proclaimed to the army: "Comrades in arms," he said, "our most sacred duties have brought us to these uninhabited lands and demand our engaging in combat against a rabble of wretched adventurers to whom our authorities have unwisely given benefits that even Mexicans did not enjoy, and who have taken possession of this vast and fertile area, convinced that our own unfortunate internal divisions have rendered us incapable of defending our soil. Wretches! Soon will they become aware of their folly! Soldiers, our comrades have been shamefully sacrificed at Anáhuac, Goliad, and Béjar, and you are those destined to punish these murderers. My friends: we will march as long as the interests of the nation that we serve demand. The claimants to the acres of Texas land will soon know to their sorrow that their reinforcements from New Orleans, Mobile, Boston, New York, and other points north, whence they should never have come, are insignificant, and that Mexicans, generous by nature, will not leave unpunished affronts resulting in injury or discredit to their country, regardless of who the aggressors may be."

This address was received enthusiastically, but the army needed no incitement; knowing that it was about to engage in the defense of the country and to avenge less fortunate comrades was enough for its ardor to become as great as the noble and just cause it was about to defend. Several officers from the Aldama and Toluca sappers were filled with joy and congratulated each other when they were ordered to hasten their march, for they knew that they were about to engage in combat. There is no doubt that some would have regretted not being among the first to meet the enemy, for it was considered an honor to be counted among the first. For their part, the enemy leaders had addressed their own men in terms not unlike those of our commander. They said that we were a bunch of mercenaries, blind instruments of tyranny; that without any right we were about to invade their territory; that we would bring desolation

and death to their peaceful homes and would seize their possessions; that we were savage men who would rape their women, decapitate their children, destroy everything, and render into ashes the fruits of their industry and their efforts. Unfortunately they did partially foresee what would happen, but they also committed atrocities that we did not commit, and in this rivalry of evil and extermination, I do not dare to venture who had the ignominious advantage, they or we!

In spirited and vehement language, they called on their compatriots to defend the interests so dear to them and those they so tenderly cherished. They urged mothers to arm their sons, and wives not to admit their consorts in their nuptial beds until they had taken up arms and risked their lives in defense of their families. The word liberty was constantly repeated in every line of their writings; this magical word was necessary to inflame the hearts of the men, who rendered tribute to this goddess, although not to the degree they pretend.

When our commander in chief haughtily rejected the agreement that the enemy had proposed, Travis became infuriated at the contemptible manner in which he had been treated and, expecting no honorable way of salvation, chose the path that strong souls choose in crisis, that of dying with honor, and selected the Alamo for his grave. It is possible that this might have been his first resolve, for although he was awaiting the reinforcements promised him,[1] he must have reflected that he would be engaged in battle before these could join him, since it would be difficult for him to cover their entry into the fort with the small force at his disposal. However, this was not the case, for about sixty men did enter one night, the only help that came. They passed through our lines unnoticed until it was too late. My opinion is reinforced by the certainty that Travis could have managed to escape during the first nights, when vigilance was much less, but this he refused to do. It has been said that General Ramírez y Sesma's division

---

1. Fannin was still expected to come with aid from Goliad. Not until several days after the Alamo fell was he ordered to Victoria instead.

was not sufficient to have formed a circumventing line on the first day, since the Alamo is a small place, one of its sides fronting the San Antonio River and clear and open fields. The heroic language in which Travis addressed his compatriots during the days of the conflict finally proved that he had resolved to die before abandoning the Alamo or surrendering unconditionally.

QUESTIONS

1. How does Santa Anna characterize the mission of the Mexican Army?
2. How does this compare to the language that de la Peña attributes to the American commanders?
3. Who does de la Peña blame for the atrocities that occurred at the Alamo and the war in general?

11.5. AMY MELENDA GALUSHA, LETTER TO AARON LELAND GALUSHA (APRIL 3, 1849)

The textile mills in Lowell, Massachusetts, housed one of the first large-scale industrial facilities in the United States. Many of the workers in the factory were young women.

Lowell, April 3, 1849

Dear Brother,

I do not know but you will blame me for not answering youre kind letter sooner but I think you will excuse me when I tell you the reason which is this I have been very sick with the vere Loyd[2] I do not know as you will know what that is so I will tell you it is the same as the small pox only it does not go quite so hard on account of being evaxionated[3] I was at the Hospital one week and I was sick enough I can tell you my face was swolen so that if you had seen me you would not have known me from Adam but I am getting pretty smart again I am not sorry that I have had it now it is over for I shall not fear the small pox any more but I had a pretty hard time I think I shall go to work again next week I expect my sickness will cost me about 15 dollers time and all which is quite

a sum as low as wages are now you wanted I should write about mens wages in the mill mens wages are good but boys wages very low I do not think it will be best for you to try to work in the mill you will have to work a good many years before you will be a capable overseer and none but such can get good wages if you go into the mill now you will have to be very steady and I know that youre disposition will not admit of youre being confined from 5 in the morning till 7 at night in a noisey factory and luging around a great basket of bobbins you would soon get tired of that fun I will promise you and then you must put up with a great many things which you never had to put up with before you would probably get scolded sometimes and that you know that you would not bear very patiently which would make it all the worse for you you would soom get weary and discontented and then you would

---

Source: Galusha Family Collection, Lowell National Historical Park, Center for Lowell History, University of Massachusetts Lowell Libraries, http://library.uml.edu/clh/All/Gal.htm.

2. Varioloid.
3. Vaccinated.

not be much better off for what you had done a boy canot get along so easy in the mill with their work as the girls do with theirs for it is harder to learn it the girls have nothing to do but tend the work after it is all fixed and set to going the men have to keep the looms and machinery in order and put in the webs [—] and fix them all in order for weaving before the girls have anything to do with it which makes the mens work more trying and more particular a great deal than the girls when I come home I will tell you all about it more than I can write I should be very glad to have you here whare I can see you but I know in all reason Lele[4] it will not be for your best interest I think the best thing that you can do will be to go into some country town and learn a good trade get into some respectable shop and be steady and industrious and do what you think is perfectly right take youre bible keep it by you where you can get at it handy read a portion of it every day and follow its precepts every day be considerate in everything if any one asks you to do a thing stop and think if it is right you can easely tell whether a thing is right or wrong by stopping to to think if you think it is wrong tell them at once that it is not right and that you will not do it and let that be the last of it do not stop to argue the point at all for they may be better skilled in argument then you are and by that I means you may weaken a strong point if you think it is wrong say so and that will be enough be independent do not be persuaded by any one however smart or rich or influential to do a wrong action you have a good mind enough for anybody if you will be guided by that do not let the evil spirit get the uper hand at any time if you can—t decide upon any question yourself go to someone that you know to be good for advise do not associate with any whose character is the least doubtful of either sex especialy the oposite Lealand for heavens sake let no fancy get the uper hands of reason do not be too ardent an admirer of outside apearances if you are attracted by a beautiful form or face stop and consider watch the actions and words with a jealous eye see if retiring modesty reigns there see if [*torn area*] place of

all [*torn area*] of folly and frivalous actions there is anything like common sense to guide the bark or if its frail and delicate form is left pilotless upon the vast ocean of time to be driven by the winds of pride and folly to the gulf of distruction Leland I think of you a great deal and tremble for youre welfare for many a boy has been ruined when young by keeping bad company but my sheet (is almost full or I might say quite full you must answer my letter as soon as you receive it give my love to [JC] and [—ll] write to them soon write soon).

(Write as soon as you receive this I heard from Canada last night Jane Westover come down and Mrs Stark).

Amy L. Galusha

(dear Lele be kind to pa an ma do not do any thing to greive or hurt their feelings for you do not know how much they feel for youre welfare Lele the world is cold pitiless and miserliy what I have suffered no one knows but I have lived to find a calm a blessed calm in a land of strangers I know that youre feelings are tender like as mine were and capable of believing the insinuations of heartless wretches who will deceive you and then expose every little word and action and egreavate it to the highest pitch put no confidence in any one however friendly they may appear until you have thoroughly proved them).

(give my love to [—] enquiring friends give my love to Aunt I and L and J and all uncle Bens folks).

(you must not show this letter to any body except ma or pa it is written from the fountain of an overflowing and affectionate heart and must not be exposed to the scorn of an unfeeling world).

QUESTIONS

1. How does Amy compare the advantages and disadvantages of millwork for men and women?
2. What values does she believe a man should possess?
3. What kind of emotional relationship does Amy seem to have with her brother?

---

4. A nickname for Aaron Leland Galusha.

CHAPTER 12

RELIGION AND REFORM, 1820 TO 1850

12.1 DAVID WALKER, "PREAMBLE" FROM APPEAL TO THE COLORED CITIZENS OF THE WORLD (1829)

David Walker was a free man of color born in 1796 to a free mother and enslaved father in North Carolina. He moved to Philadelphia and then Boston in the 1820s, where he worked selling secondhand clothes to sailors. He was active in the campaign against slavery, wrote for *Freedom's Journal*, the first African American owned newspaper in the U.S., and in 1829 published the *Appeal*.

Having travelled over a considerable portion of these United States, and having, in the course of my travels taken the most accurate observations of things as they exist—the result of my observations has warranted the full and unshakened conviction, that we, (colored people of these United States) are the most degraded, wretched, and abject set of beings that ever lived since the world began, and I pray God, that none like us ever may live again until time shall be no more. They tell us of the Israelites in Egypt, the Helots in Sparta, and of the Roman Slaves, which last, were made up from almost every nation under heaven, whose sufferings under those ancient and heathen nations were, in comparison with ours, under this enlightened and Christian nation, no more than a cypher—or in other words, those heathen nations of antiquity, had but little more among them than the name and form of slavery, while wretchedness and endless miseries were reserved, apparently in a phial, to be poured out upon our fathers, ourselves and our children by Christian Americans!

[. . .]

I am fully aware, in making this appeal to my much afflicted and suffering brethren, that I shall not only be assailed by those whose greatest earthly desires are, to keep us in abject ignorance and wretchedness, and who are of the firm conviction that Heaven has designed us and our children to be slaves and *beasts*

Source: *http://docsouth.unc.edu/nc/walker/walker.html*

of burden to them and their children. I say, I do not only expect to be held up to the public as an ignorant, impudent and restless disturber of the public peace, by such avaricious creatures, as well as a mover of insubordination—and perhaps put in prison or to death, for giving a superficial exposition of our miseries, and exposing tyrants . . . But against all accusations which may or can be preferred against me, I appeal to Heaven for my motive in writing—who knows that my object is, if possible, to awaken in the breasts of my afflicted, degraded and slumbering brethren, a spirit of inquiry and investigation respecting our miseries and wretchedness in this *Republican Land of Liberty! ! ! ! ! !*

[. . .]

And as the inhuman system of *slavery*, is the *source* from which most of our miseries proceed, I shall begin with that *curse to nations*, which has spread terror and devastation through so many nations of antiquity, and which is raging to such a pitch at the present day in Spain and in Portugal. It had one tug in England, in France, and in the United States of America; yet the inhabitants thereof, do not learn wisdom, and erase it entirely from their dwellings and from all with whom they have to do. The fact is, the labour of slaves comes so cheap to the avaricious usurpers, and is (as they think) of such great utility to the country where it exists, that those who are actuated by sordid avarice only, overlook the evils, which will as sure as the Lord lives, follow after the good. In fact, they are so happy to keep in ignorance and degradation, and to receive the homage and the labour of the slaves, they forget that God rules in the armies of heaven and among the inhabitants of the earth, having his ears continually open to the cries, tears and groans of his oppressed people; and being a just and holy Being will at one day appear fully in behalf of the oppressed, and arrest the progress of the avaricious oppressors

[. . .]

I say, I shall not take up time to speak of the *causes* which produced so much wretchedness and massacre among those heathen nations, for I am aware that you know too well, that God is just, as well as merciful!—I shall call your attention a few moments to that *Christian* nation, the Spaniards—while I shall leave almost unnoticed, that avaricious and cruel people, the Portuguese, among whom all true hearted Christians and lovers of Jesus Christ, must evidently see the judgments of God displayed. To show the judgments of God upon the Spaniards, I shall occupy but a little time, leaving a plenty of room for the candid and unprejudiced to reflect.

All persons who are acquainted with history, and particularly the Bible, who are not blinded by the God of this world, and are not actuated solely by avarice—who are able to lay aside prejudice long enough to view candidly and impartially, things as they were, are, and probably will be—who are willing to admit that God made man to serve Him *alone,* and that man should have no other Lord or Lords but Himself—that God Almighty is the *sole proprietor* or *master* of the WHOLE human family, and will not on any consideration admit of a colleague, being unwilling to divide his glory with another—and who can dispense with prejudice long enough to admit that we are *men,* notwithstanding our *improminent noses* and *woolly heads,* and believe that we feel for our fathers, mothers, wives and children, as well as the whites do for theirs.—I say, all who are permitted to see and believe these things, can easily recognize the judgments of God among the Spaniards. Though others may lay the cause of the fierceness with which they cut each other's throats, to some other circumstance, yet they who believe that God is a God of justice, will believe that SLAVERY *is the principal cause.I*

QUESTIONS

1. What arguments does Walker make against slavery?
2. How does Walker's *Appeal* engage with the ideas or language of the Second Great Awakening?
3. How does Walker use global history to inspire action against slavery?

12.2. VISUAL DOCUMENT: WOODCUT, "A HORRID MASSACRE" (1831)

In 1831, Nat Turner, an enslaved man, led a slave revolt in Southampton County, Virginia. Turner used his experience as a preacher to the county's slaves to create a network of lieutenants and plan the attack. His group killed 56 white people but could not seize the county armory before the local militia counterattacked and dispersed them. Turner was later captured and executed. The woodcut shown here circulated widely in Virginia newspapers.

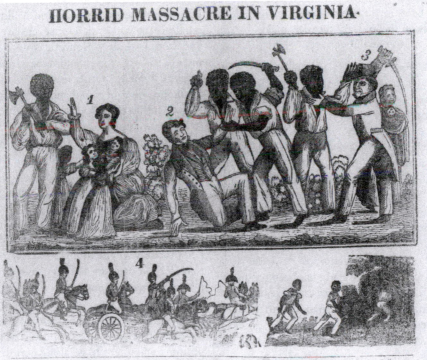

QUESTIONS

1. How does the author of this woodcut represent blacks and whites as individuals?
2. How does the difference in weapons suggest attitudes about the positions of black and white men in the society?
3. How does the bottom sequence present the organization and intent of the two sides in the struggle?

Source: F&A Archive/The Art Archive at Art Resource, NYImage.

12.3. CHARLES G. FINNEY, EXCERPTS FROM "WHAT A REVIVAL OF RELIGION IS" (1835)

Charles Finney was one of the leading ministers of the Second Great Awakening, a religious revival movement that occurred during the 1820s and 1830s. Originally a Presbyterian, Finney preached a widely accessible evangelical Christian message intended to create converts and energize believers to improve their own behavior and their society.

TEXT.—O Lord, revive thy work in the midst of the years, in the midst of the years make known; in wrath remember mercy. —HAB. iii. 2.

Religion is the work of man. It is something for man to do. It consists in obeying God with and from the heart. It is man's duty. It is true, God induces him to do it. He influences him by his Spirit, because of his great wickedness and reluctance to obey. If it were not necessary for God to influence men—if men were disposed to obey God, there would be no occasion to pray, "O Lord, revive thy work." The ground of necessity for such a prayer is, that men are wholly indisposed to obey; and unless God interpose the influence of his Spirit, not a man on earth will ever obey the commands of God.

A "Revival of Religion" presupposes a declension. Almost all the religion in the world has been produced by revivals. God has found it necessary to take advantage of the excitability there is in mankind, to produce powerful excitements among them, before he can lead them to obey. Men are so spiritually sluggish, there are so many things to lead their minds off from religion, and to oppose the influence of the Gospel, that it is necessary to raise an excitement among them, till the tide rises so high as to sweep away the opposing obstacles. They must be so excited that they will break over these counteracting influences, before they will obey God. Not that excited feeling is religion, for it is not; but

it is excited desire, appetite and feeling that prevents religion. The will is, in a sense, enslaved by the carnal and worldly desires. Hence it is necessary to awaken men to a sense of guilt and danger, and thus produce an excitement of counter feeling and desire which will break the power of carnal and worldly desire and leave the will free to obey God. . . . There is so little principle in the church, so little firmness and stability of purpose, that unless the religious feelings are awakened and kept excited, counter worldly feeling and excitement will prevail, and men will not obey God. They have so little knowledge, and their principles are so weak, that unless they are excited, they will go back from the path of duty, and do nothing to promote the glory of God. The state of the world is still such, and probably will be till the millennium is fully come, that religion must be mainly promoted by means of revivals. How long and how often has the experiment been tried, to bring the church to act steadily for God, without these periodical excitements. Many good men have supposed, and still suppose, that the best way to promote religion, is to go along uniformly, and gather in the ungodly gradually, and without excitement. But however sound such reasoning may appear in the abstract, facts demonstrate its futility. If the church were far enough advanced in knowledge, and had stability of principle enough to keep awake, such a course would do; but the church is so little enlightened, and

Source: Lectures on the Revivals of Religion Delivered by the Rev. Charles G. Finney, rev. ed. (Oberlin, Ohio: E. J. Goodrich, 1868). Also see http://www.gospeltruth.net/1868Lect_on_Rev_of_Rel/68revlec01.htm.

there are so many counteracting causes, that she will not go steadily to work without a special interest being awakened. As the millennium advances, it is probable that these periodical excitements will be unknown. Then the church will be enlightened, and the counteracting causes removed, and the entire church will be in a state of habitual and steady obedience to God. The entire church will stand and take the infant mind, and cultivate it for God. Children will be trained up in the way they should go, and there will be no such torrents of worldliness, and fashion, and covetousness, to bear away the piety of the church, as soon as the excitement of a revival is withdrawn. . . .

Backslidden Christians will be brought to repentance. A revival is nothing else than a new beginning of obedience to God. Just as in the case of a converted sinner, the first step is a deep repentance, a breaking down of heart, a getting down into the dust before God, with deep humility, and forsaking of sin. . . .

Christians will have their faith renewed. While they are in their backslidden state they are blind to the state of sinners. Their hearts are as hard as marble. The truths of the Bible only appear like a dream. They admit it to be all true; their conscience and their judgment assent to it; but their faith does not see it standing out in bold relief, in all the burning realities of eternity. But when they enter into a revival, they no longer see men as trees walking, but they see things in that strong light which will renew the love of God in their hearts. This will lead them to labor zealously to bring others to him. They will feel grieved that others do not love God, when they love him so much. And they will set themselves feelingly to persuade their neighbors to give him their hearts. So their love to men will be renewed. They will be filled with a tender and burning love for souls. They will have a longing desire for the salvation of the whole world. They will be in an agony for individuals whom they want to have saved—their friends, relations, enemies. They will not only be urging them to give their hearts to God, but they will carry them to God in the arms of faith, and with strong crying and tears beseech God to

have mercy on them, and save their souls from endless burnings. . . .

FINALLY. —I have a proposal to make to you who are here present. I have not commenced this course of Lectures on Revivals to get up a curious theory of my own on the subject. I would not spend my time and strength merely to give you instructions, to gratify your curiosity, and furnish you something to talk about. I have no idea of preaching about revivals. It is not my design to preach so as to have you able to say at the close, "We understand all about revivals now," while you do nothing. But I wish to ask you a question. What do you hear lectures on revivals for? Do you mean that whenever you are convinced what your duty is in promoting a revival, you will go to work and practise it?

Will you follow the instructions I shall give you from the word of God, and put them in practise in your own lives? Will you bring them to bear upon your families, your acquaintance, neighbors, and through the city? Or will you spend the winter in learning about revivals, and do nothing for them? I want you, as fast as you learn any thing on the subject of revivals, to put it in practice, and go to work and see if you cannot promote a revival among sinners here. If you will not do this, I wish you to let me know at the beginning, so that I need not waste my strength. You ought to decide now whether you will do this or not. You know that we call sinners to decide on the spot whether they will obey the Gospel. And we have no more authority to let you take time to deliberate whether you will obey God, than we have to let sinners do so. We call on you to unite now in a solemn pledge to God, that you will do your duty as fast as you learn what it is, and to pray that He will pour out his Spirit upon this church and upon all the city this winter.

QUESTIONS

1. What is Finney's critique of the established Christian churches?
2. What does Finney ask of his listeners?
3. How might people converted in this manner engage with public problems?

12.4. ELIZABETH CADY STANTON, "DECLARATION OF SENTIMENTS" (1848)

This document was primarily written by Elizabeth Cady Stanton, a leading activist for the full citizenship of women. Passed at the Seneca Falls Convention in 1848, Stanton modeled her document after the Declaration of Independence.

When, in the course of human events, it becomes necessary for one portion of the family of man to assume among the people of the earth a position different from that which they have hitherto occupied, but one to which the laws of nature and of nature's God entitle them, a decent respect to the opinions of mankind requires that they should declare the causes that impel them to such a course.

We hold these truths to be self-evident: that all men and women are created equal; that they are endowed by their Creator with certain inalienable rights; that among these are life, liberty, and the pursuit of happiness; that to secure these rights governments are instituted, deriving their just powers from the consent of the governed. Whenever any form of government becomes destructive of these ends, it is the right of those who suffer from it to refuse allegiance to it, and to insist upon the institution of a new government, laying its foundation on such principles, and organizing its powers in such form, as to them shall seem most likely to effect their safety and happiness. Prudence, indeed, will dictate that governments long established should not be changed for light and transient causes; and accordingly all experience hath shown that mankind are more disposed to suffer, while evils are sufferable, than to right themselves by abolishing the forms to which they were accustomed. But when a long train of abuses and usurpations, pursuing invariably the same object evinces a design to reduce them under absolute despotism, it is their duty to throw off such government, and to provide new guards for their future security. Such has been the patient sufferance of the women under this government, and such is now the necessity which constrains them to demand the equal station to which they are entitled.

The history of mankind is a history of repeated injuries and usurpations on the part of man toward woman, having in direct object the establishment of an absolute tyranny over her. To prove this, let facts be submitted to a candid world.

He has never permitted her to exercise her inalienable right to the elective franchise.

He has compelled her to submit to laws, in the formation of which she had no voice.

He has withheld from her rights which are given to the most ignorant and degraded men—both natives and foreigners.

Having deprived her of this first right of a citizen, the elective franchise, thereby leaving her without representation in the halls of legislation, he has oppressed her on all sides.

He has made her, if married, in the eye of the law, civilly dead.

He has taken from her all right in property, even to the wages she earns.

He has made her, morally, an irresponsible being, as she can commit many crimes with impunity, provided they be done in the presence of her husband. In the covenant of marriage, she is compelled to promise obedience to her husband, he becoming, to all intents and purposes, her master—the law giving him power to deprive her of her liberty, and to administer chastisement.

Source: Elizabeth Cady Stanton, Susan B. Anthony, and Matilda Joslyn Gage, eds., *History of Woman Suffrage* (Rochester, N.Y.: Charles Mann, 1887), 70–71.

He has so framed the laws of divorce, as to what shall be the proper causes, and in case of separation, to whom the guardianship of the children shall be given, as to be wholly regardless of the happiness of women—the law, in all cases, going upon a false supposition of the supremacy of man, and giving all power into his hands.

After depriving her of all rights as a married woman, if single, and the owner of property, he has taxed her to support a government which recognizes her only when her property can be made profitable to it.

He has monopolized nearly all the profitable employments, and from those she is permitted to follow, she receives but a scanty remuneration. He closes against her all the avenues to wealth and distinction which he considers most honorable to himself. As a teacher of theology, medicine, or law, she is not known.

He has denied her the facilities for obtaining a thorough education, all colleges being closed against her.

He allows her in Church, as well as State, but a subordinate position, claiming Apostolic authority for her exclusion from the ministry, and, with some exceptions, from any public participation in the affairs of the Church.

He has created a false public sentiment by giving to the world a different code of morals for men and women, by which moral delinquencies which exclude women from society, are not only tolerated, but deemed of little account in man.

He has usurped the prerogative of Jehovah himself, claiming it as his right to assign for her a sphere of action, when that belongs to her conscience and to her God.

He has endeavored, in every way that he could, to destroy her confidence in her own powers, to lessen her self-respect, and to make her willing to lead a dependent and abject life.

Now, in view of this entire disfranchisement of one-half the people of this country, their social and religious degradation—in view of the unjust laws above mentioned, and because women do feel themselves aggrieved, oppressed, and fraudulently deprived of their most sacred rights, we insist that they have immediate admission to all the rights and privileges which belong to them as citizens of the United States.

In entering upon the great work before us, we anticipate no small amount of misconception, misrepresentation, and ridicule; but we shall use every instrumentality within our power to effect our object. We shall employ agents, circulate tracts, petition the State and National legislatures, and endeavor to enlist the pulpit and the press in our behalf. We hope this Convention will be followed by a series of Conventions embracing every part of the country.

QUESTIONS

1. What are the chief criticisms that this document makes regarding the treatment of women in 1840s America?
2. What is the effect of Stanton's decision to copy the language of the Declaration of Independence?
3. How would Americans in the 1840s have interpreted this comparison?

12.5. WALT WHITMAN, *ONE'S SELF I SING* (1871)

The rise of an authentic American literature accelerated in the 1840s and 1850s as figures such as Nathaniel Hawthorne, Emily Dickinson, Herman Melville, and Walt Whitman wrote some of their most famous works. Whitman pioneered the use of free verse and an attention to the lived experience of citizens from all walks of his life. His frank discussions of sexuality and body alienated and energized equal numbers of readers.

One's-self I sing, a simple separate person,
Yet utter the word Democratic, the word
    En-Masse.

Of physiology from top to toe I sing,
Not physiognomy alone nor brain alone is wor-
    thy for the
Muse, I say the Form complete is worthier far,
The Female equally with the Male I sing.

Of Life immense in passion, pulse, and power,
Cheerful, for freest action form'd under the laws
    divine,
The Modern Man I sing.

QUESTIONS

1. How does Whitman present the idea of individualism?
2. What kind of person is the "modern" American, according to Whitman?
3. Is this poem an argument for gender equality?

CHAPTER 13

A HOUSE DIVIDING, 1844 TO 1860

13.1 VISUAL DOCUMENT: GEORGE CATLIN, *COMANCHE FEATS OF HORSEMANSHIP* (1834)

Born in Pennsylvania, Catlin made himself the most well-known and well-regarded artist of Indian life in the United States. He traveled extensively in the West throughout the 1830s and completed many portraits of chiefs and members of Western tribes. Although Catlin clearly posed his subjects and created art, he also considered his work a chronicle of the people and material life of American Indians.

Source: George Catlin, "Comanche Feats of Horsemanship," 1834. Smithsonian American Art Museum.

QUESTIONS

1. What does the painting convey about Comanche martial skill?

2. How does the artist's representation of Comanche bodies reflect attitudes about differences between Indian and European men?

13.2. EXCERPT FROM ARTICLE 11, TREATY OF GUADALUPE HIDALGO (FEBRUARY 2, 1848)

The Treaty of Guadalupe Hidalgo ended the U.S.–Mexican War. It provided for the withdrawal of American troops from occupied Mexican cities and forts and established a new international boundary between the two nations. One of the treaty's articles (Article XI) concerned the ongoing problem of Indian raids (principally Apache) into northern Mexico.

Considering that a great part of the territories, which, by the present treaty, are to be comprehended for the future within the limits of the United States, is now occupied by savage tribes, who will hereafter be under the exclusive control of the Government of the United States, and whose incursions within the territory of Mexico would be prejudicial in the extreme, it is solemnly agreed that all such incursions shall be forcibly restrained by the Government of the United States whensoever this may be necessary; and that when they cannot be prevented, they shall be punished by the said Government, and satisfaction for the same shall be exacted all in the same way, and with equal diligence and energy, as if the same incursions were meditated or committed within its own territory, against its own citizens.

It shall not be lawful, under any pretext whatever, for any inhabitant of the United States to purchase or acquire any Mexican, or any foreigner residing in Mexico, who may have been captured by Indians inhabiting the territory of either of the two republics; nor to purchase or acquire horses, mules, cattle, or property of any kind, stolen within Mexican territory by such Indians.

And in the event of any person or persons, captured within Mexican territory by Indians, being carried into the territory of the United States, the Government of the latter engages and binds itself, in the most solemn manner, so soon as it shall know of such captives being within its territory, and shall be able so to do, through the faithful exercise of its influence and power, to rescue them and return them to their country. or deliver them to the agent or representative of the Mexican Government. The Mexican authorities will, as far as practicable, give to the Government of the United States notice of such captures; and its agents shall pay the expenses incurred in the maintenance and transmission of the rescued captives; who, in the mean time, shall be treated with the utmost hospitality by the American authorities at the place where they may be. But if the Government of the United States, before receiving such notice from Mexico, should obtain intelligence, through any other channel, of the existence of Mexican captives within its territory, it will proceed forthwith to effect their release and delivery to the Mexican agent, as above stipulated.

Source: http://avalon.law.yale.edu/19th_century/guadhida.asp

QUESTIONS

1. What does the inclusion of this clause suggest about the stability of the northern Mexico border in the years before the war?

2. How might requiring the U.S. government to police the boundary create future problems for the independence of the Mexican government?

3. What does the treaty language suggest about American and Mexican attitudes toward the native people of the region?

13.3. GOVERNOR JAMES HENRY HAMMOND, EXCERPTS FROM A LETTER TO THOMAS CLARKSON (1845)

Hammond served as governor and senator for South Carolina in the 1840s and 1850s. He emerged as one of the most vigorous defenders of slavery and the Southern social order. The document here, a response to the English abolitionist Thomas Clarkson's critique of Southern slavery, circulated widely in the United States and Britain.

Let us . . . turn to American slavery, to which you have now directed your attention, and against which a crusade has been preached as enthusiastic and ferocious as that of Peter the Hermit—destined, I believe, to be about as successful. And here let me say, there is not a vast difference between the two, though you may not acknowledge it. The wisdom of ages has concurred in the justice and expediency of establishing rights by prescriptive use, however tortious in their origin they may have been. You would deem a man insane whose keen sense of equity would lead him to denounce your right to the lands you hold, and which perhaps you inherited from a long line of ancestry, because your title was derived from a Saxon or Norman conqueror, and your lands were originally wrested by violence from the vanquished Britons. And so would the New England Abolitionist regard any one who would insist that he should restore his farm to the descendants of the slaughtered Red men, to whom, God has as clearly given it, as he gave life and freedom to the kidnapped African. That time does not consecrate wrong, is a fallacy which all history exposes; and which the best and wisest men of all ages and professions of religious faith, have practically denied. The means, therefore, whatever they may have been, by which the African race now in this country, have been reduced to slavery, cannot affect us, since they are our property, as your land is yours, by inheritance or purchase and prescriptive right. You will say that man cannot hold *property in man*. The answer is, that he can, and *actually does* hold property in his fellow all the world over, in a variety of forms, and *has always done so*. I will show presently his authority for doing it.

If you were to ask me whether I was an advocate of slavery in the abstract, I should probably answer, that I am not, according to my understanding of the question. I do not like to deal in abstractions; it seldom leads to any useful ends. There are few universal truths.

Source: *Gov. Hammond's Letters on Southern Slavery: Addressed to Thomas Clarkson, the English Abolitionist* (Charleston: Walker and Burke, 1845).

I do not now remember any single moral truth universally acknowledged. We have no assurance that it is given to our finite understanding to comprehend abstract moral truth. Apart from Revelation and the Inspired writings, what ideas should we have even of God, Salvation and Immortality? Let the Heathen answer. Justice itself is impalpable as an abstraction, and abstract liberty the merest phantasy that ever amused the imagination. This world was made for man, and man for the world as it is. Ourselves, our relations with one another, and with all matter, are real, not ideal. I might say that I am no more in favor of slavery in the abstract, than I am of pover[t]y, disease, deformity, idiocy or any other inequality in the condition of the human family; that I love perfection, and think I should enjoy a Millenium such as God has promised. But what would it amount to? A pledge that I would join you to set about eradicating those apparently inevitable evils of our nature, in equalizing the condition of all mankind, consummating the perfection of our race, and introducing the Millenium? By no means. To effect these things belongs exclusively to a higher power, and would be well for us to leave the Almighty to perfect His own works and fulfil His own covenants. Especially, as the history of all the past shows how entirely futile all human efforts have proved, when made for the purpose of aiding Him in carrying out even His revealed designs, and how invarially he has accomplished them by unconscious instruments, and in the face of human expectation. Nay more, that every attempt which has been made by fallible man to extort from the world obedience to his "abstract" notions of right and wrong, has been invariably attended with calamities, dire and extended, just in proportion to the breadth and vigor of the movement. On slavery in the abstract then, it would not be amiss to have as little as possible to say. Let us contemplate it as it is. And thus contemplating it, the first question we have to ask ourselves is, whether it is contrary to the Will of God, as revealed to us in His holy scriptures—the only certain means given us to ascertain His will. If it is, then slavery is a sin; and I admit at once that every man is bound to set his face against it, and to emancipate his slaves, should he hold any. . . .

I think, then, I may safely conclude, and I firmly believe, that American slavery is not only not a sin, but especially commanded by God through Moses, and approved by Christ through his apostles. And here I might close its defence; for what God ordained and Christ sanctifies, should surely command the respect and toleration of man. But I fear there has grown up in our time a Transcendental Religion which is throwing even Transcendental Philosophy into the shade; a religion too pure and elevated for the Bible; which seeks to erect among men a higher standard of morals than the Almighty has revealed or our Saviour preached, and which is probably destined to do more to impede the extension of God's Kingdom on earth than all the Infidels who have ever lived. Error is error. It is as dangerous to deviate to the right hand as to the left. And when men professing to be holy men, and who are by numbers so regarded, declare those things to be sinful which our Creator has expressly authorized and instituted, they do more to destroy his authority among mankind than the most wicked can affect by proclaiming that to be innocent which He has forbidden. To this self-righteous and self-exalted class belong all the Abolitionists whose writings I have read. With them it is no end of the argument to prove your propositions by the test of the Bible, interpreted according to its plain and palpable meaning, and as understood by all mankind for three thousand years before their time. They are more ingenious in construing and interpolating to accommodate it to their new-fangled and etherial code of morals, than ever were Voltaire or Hume in picking it to pieces to free the world from what they considered a delusion. When the Abolitionists proclaim "man-stealing" to be a sin, and show me that it is so written down by God, I admit them to be right, and shudder at the idea of such a crime. But when I show them that to hold "bond-men forever" is ordained by God, *they deny the Bible, and set up in its place a Law of their own making.* I must then cease to reason with them on this branch of the question. Our religion differs as widely as our manners. The Great Judge in our day of final account must decide between us. . . . I indorse without reserve, the much abused sentiment of Gov. M'Duffie, that "slavery is the corner stone of our republican edifice;" while I repudiate, as ridiculously absurd, that much lauded but no where accredited dogma, of Mr. Jefferson, that "all men are born equal." No Society has ever yet existed, and I have already incidentally quoted the highest authority to show that none ever will exist, without a natural variety of classes. The most marked of these must in a country like ours, be the rich and the poor, the educated and the ignorant. It will scarcely be disputed that the very poor have less leisure to prepare themselves for the proper discharge of public duties than the rich; and that the ignorant are wholly unfit for them at all. In all countries save ours, these two classes, or the poor rather, who are presumed to be necessarily ignorant, are by law expressly excluded from all participation in the management of public affairs. In a repudlican [*sic*] Government this cannot be done. Universal suffrage, though not essential in theory, seems to be in fact, a necessary appendage to a republican system. Where universal suffrage obtains, it is obvious that the Government is in the hands of a numerical majority: and it is hardly necessary to say, that in every part of the world more than half the people are ignorant and poor. Though no one can look upon poverty as a crime, and we do not generally here regard it as any objection to a man in his individual capacity, still it must be admitted that it is a wretched and insecure government which is administered by its most ignorant citizens, and those who have the least at stake under it. Though intelligence and wealth have great influence here as everywhere, in keeping in check reckless and unenlightened numbers, yet it is evident to close observers, if not to all, that these are rapidly usurping all power in the non-slave-holding States, and threaten a fearful crisis in Republican Institutious [*sic*] there at no remote period. In the slave-holding States, however, nearly one half of the whole population, and those the poorest and most ignorant, have no political influence whatever, because they are slaves. Of the other half, a large proportion are both educated and independent in their circumstances, while those who unfortunately are not so, being still elevated far above the mass, are higher toned and more deeply interested in preserving a stable and well ordered government, than the same class in any other country. Hence, slavery is truly the "corner stone" and foundation of every well designed and durable "Republican edifice." . . . I have yet to reply to the main ground on which you and your coadjutors rely for the overthrow of our system of slavery. Failing in all your attempts to prove that it is sinful in its nature, immoral in its effects, a political evil, and profitless to those who maintain it, you appeal to the sympathies of mankind, and attempt to arouse the world against us by the most shocking charges of tyranny and cruelty. You begin by a vehement denunciation of "the irresponsible power of one man over his fellowmen." The question of the responsibility of power is a vast one. It is the great political question of modern times. Whole nations divide off upon it and establish different fundamental systems of government. That "responsibility," which to one set of millions seems amply sufficient to check the government, to the support of which they devote their lives and fortunes, appears to another set of millions a mere mockery of restraint. And accordingly as the opinions of these millions differ, they honor each other with the epithets of "Serfs" or "Anarchists." It is ridiculous to introduce such an idea as this into the discussion of a mere Domestic Institution. But since you have introduced it, I deny that the power of the slaveholder in America is "irresponsible." He is responsible to God. He is responsible to the world—a responsibility which Abolitionists do not intend to allow him to evade—and in acknowledgment of which I write you this letter. He is responsible to the community in which he lives, and to the laws under which he enjoys his civil rights. Those laws do not permit him to kill, to maim, or to punish beyond certain limits, or to overtask or to refuse to feed and clothe his slave. In short, they forbid him to be tyrannical or cruel. If any of those laws have grown obsolete, it is because they are so seldom violated that they are forgotten. You have disinterred one of them from a compilation by some Judge STROUD, of Philapelphia [*sic*], to stigmatize its inadequate penalties for killing, maiming, &c. Your objects appears to be—you can have no other—to produce the impression that it must be often violated on account of its insufficiency. You say as much, and that it marks our estimate of the slave. You forget to state that this law was enacted by *Englishmen*, and only indicates *their* opinion of the reparation due for these offences. Ours is proved by the fact, though perhaps unknown to Judge STROUD or yourself, that we have essentially altered this law; and the murder of a slave has for many years been punishable with death in this State. And so it is, I believe, in most or all the slave States. You seem well aware, however, that laws have been recently passed in all these States making it penal to teach slaves to read. Do you know what occasioned their passage, and renders their stringent enforcement necessary. I can tell you: it was the abolition agitation. If the slave is not allowed to read his Bible, the sin rests upon the Abolitionists; for they stand prepared to furnish him with a key to it, which would make it, not a book of hope and love and peace, but of despair, hatred and blood; which would convert the reader, not into a Christian, but a Demon. To preserve him from such a horrid destiny, it is a sacred duty which we owe to slaves, not less than to ourselves, to interpose the most decisive means. If the Catholics deem it wrong to trust the Bible to the hands of ignorance, shall we be excommunicated because we will not give and with it the corrupt and fatal commentaries of the Abolitionists, to our slaves? Allow our slaves to read your pamphlets, stimulating them to cut our throats! Can you believe us to be such unspeakable fools. . . . Is timely preparation and gradual emancipation suggested to avert these horrible consequences? I thought your experience in the West Indies had at least done so much as to explode that idea. If it failed there, much more would it fail here, where the two races, approximating to equality in numbers, are daily and hourly in the closest contact. Give room for but a single spark of real jealousy to be kindled between them, and the explosion would be instantaneous and universal. It is the most fatal of all fallacies to suppose that these two races can exist together, after any length of time or any process of preparation, on terms at all approaching to equality. Of this, both of them are finally and fixedly convinced. They differ essentially, in all the leading traits that characterise the varieties of the human species, and color draws an indelible and insuperable line of separation between them. Every scheme founded upon the idea that they can remain together on the same soil, beyond the briefest period, in any other relation than precisely that which now subsists between them, is not only preposterous, but fraught with deepest danger. If there was no alternative but to try the "experiment" here, reason and humanity dictate that the suffering of "gradualism" should be saved, and the catastrophe of "immediate abolition," enacted as rapidly as possible. Are you impatient for the performance to commence? Do you long to gloat over the scenes I have suggested, but could not hold the pen to portray? In your long life many such have passed under your review. You know that *they* are not *"impossible."* Can they be to your taste? Do you believe that in laboring to bring them about the Abolitionists are doing the will of God? No! God is not there. It is the work of Satan. The Arch-fiend, under specious guise, has found his way into your souls, and with false appeals to philanthropy, and foul insinuations to ambition, instigates them to rush headlong to the accomplishment of his diabolical designs.

QUESTIONS

1. How does Hammond distinguish between slavery in the abstract and slavery in practice?
2. What is Hammond's political argument for slavery, and why does he believe that slavery is necessary in order for democracy to function?

13.4. REPUBLICAN PARTY PLATFORM (1856)

The Republican Party emerged from the collapse of the Whig Party in the mid-1850s. It combined some of the Whig's economic development policies (and, in some cases, parts of the American Party's nativism platform) with a significant opposition to the expansion of slavery in the western territories. In 1856 for the first time Republicans ran a presidential candidate, and although he lost, Republican congressional candidates won seats all across the North.

This Convention of Delegates, assembled in pursuance of a call addressed to the people of the United States, without regard to past political differences or divisions, who are opposed to the repeal of the Missouri Compromise; to the policy of the present Administration; to the extension [of] Slavery into Free Territory; in favor of the admission of Kansas as a Free State; of restoring the action of the Federal Government to the principles of Washington and Jefferson; and for the purpose of presenting candidates for the offices of President and Vice-President, do . . . Resolved: That, with our Republican fathers, we hold it to be a self-evident truth, that all men are endowed with the inalienable right to life, liberty, and the pursuit of happiness, and that the primary object and ulterior design of our Federal Government were to secure these rights to all persons under its exclusive jurisdiction; that, as our Republican fathers, when they had abolished Slavery in all our National Territory, ordained that no person shall be deprived of life, liberty, or property, without due process of law, it becomes our duty to maintain this provision of the Constitution against all attempts to violate it for the purpose of establishing Slavery in the Territories of the United States by positive legislation, prohibiting its existence or extension therein. That we deny the authority of Congress, of a Territorial Legislation, of any individual, or association of individuals, to give legal existence to Slavery in any Territory of the United States, while the present Constitution shall be maintained.

Resolved: That the Constitution confers upon Congress sovereign powers over the Territories of the United States for their government; and that in the exercise of this power, it is both the right and the imperative duty of Congress to prohibit in the Territories those twin relics of barbarism—Polygamy, and Slavery.

Resolved: That while the Constitution of the United States was ordained and established by the people, in order to "form a more perfect union, establish justice, insure domestic tranquility, provide for the common defense, promote the general welfare, and secure the blessings of liberty," and contain ample provision for the protection of the life, liberty, and property of every citizen, the dearest Constitutional rights of the people of Kansas have been fraudulently and violently taken from them.

Their Territory has been invaded by an armed force;

Spurious and pretended legislative, judicial, and executive officers have been set over them, by whose usurped authority, sustained by the military power of the government, tyrannical and unconstitutional laws have been enacted and enforced;

The right of the people to keep and bear arms has been infringed.

Test oaths of an extraordinary and entangling nature have been imposed as a condition of exercising the right of suffrage and holding office.

The right of an accused person to a speedy and public trial by an impartial jury has been denied;

Source: http://www.ushistory.org/gop/convention_1856republicanplatform.htm.

The right of the people to be secure in their persons, houses, papers, and effects, against unreasonable searches and seizures, has been violated;

They have been deprived of life, liberty, and property without due process of law;

That the freedom of speech and of the press has been abridged;

The right to choose their representatives has been made of no effect;

Murders, robberies, and arsons have been instigated and encouraged, and the offenders have been allowed to go unpunished;

That all these things have been done with the knowledge, sanction, and procurement of the present National Administration; and that for this high crime against the Constitution, the Union, and humanity, we arraign that Administration, the President, his advisers, agents, supporters, apologists, and accessories, either before or after the fact, before the country and before the world; and that it is our fixed purpose to bring the actual perpetrators of these atrocious outrages and their accomplices to a sure and condign punishment thereafter.

Resolved, That Kansas should be immediately admitted as a state of this Union, with her present Free Constitution, as at once the most effectual way of securing to her citizens the enjoyment of the rights and privileges to which they are entitled, and of ending the civil strife now raging in her territory. . . . Resolved,

That a railroad to the Pacific Ocean by the most central and practicable route is imperatively demanded by the interests of the whole country, and that the Federal Government ought to render immediate and efficient aid in its construction, and as an auxiliary thereto, to the immediate construction of an emigrant road on the line of the railroad.

Resolved, That appropriations by Congress for the improvement of rivers and harbors, of a national character, required for the accommodation and security of our existing commerce, are authorized by the Constitution, and justified by the obligation of the Government to protect the lives and property of its citizens.

Resolved, That we invite the affiliation and cooperation of the men of all parties, however differing from us in other respects, in support of the principles herein declared; and believing that the spirit of our institutions as well as the Constitution of our country, guarantees liberty of conscience and equality of rights among citizens, we oppose all legislation impairing their security.

QUESTIONS

1. How do the Republicans root their opposition to slavery in the Constitution?
2. How does this argument differ from that of more traditional abolitionists such as Douglass?
3. Why was the condition of Kansas, where few slaves lived, so important to the Republican Party?

13.5. VICTOR HUGO, VISUAL DOCUMENT: "JOHN BROWN" (DECEMBER 2, 1859)

In 1859, John Brown, a white abolitionist, attacked the U.S. armory at Harpers Ferry, Virginia, in a failed slave revolt. Brown was executed for attempting to incite an insurrection. Victor Hugo was one of the most well-known French writers of the 19th century. He worked in a variety of forms and gained fame for his poetry, novels, and plays. Hugo evolved into an ardent republican and championed democratic movements around the world.

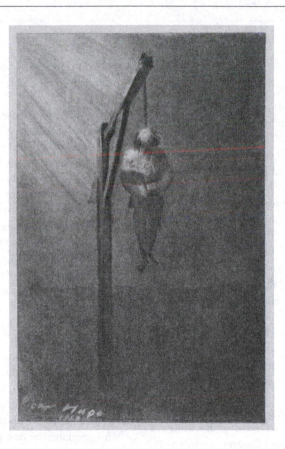

QUESTIONS

1. What does this image convey about Hugo's conception of John Brown?
2. Why is Brown represented alone, without the presence of the guards and executioner who were present?
3. What is the significance of the light that fills the upper left corner of the image?

Source: https://commons.wikimedia.org/wiki/File:John_Brown-Hugo-Chenay.jpg

13.6. STEPHEN F. HALE, EXCERPTS FROM A LETTER TO B. MAGOFFIN (DECEMBER 27, 1860)

An Alabamian, Stephen Hale had served in the U.S. Army and accepted a commission in the Confederate Army during the Civil War. In the winter of 1860–1861, Hale served as one of several "commissioners" sent by Deep South states into the Upper South to convince those states to secede. Like the other commissioners, Hale addressed a variety of public and private audiences while in Kentucky.

FRANKFORT, *December 27, 1860.*

His Excellency B. MAGOFFIN,

Governor of the Commonwealth of Kentucky:

I have the honor of placing in your hands herewith a commission from the Governor of the State of Alabama, accrediting me as a commissioner from that State to the sovereign State of Kentucky, to consult in reference to the momentous issues now pending between the Northern and Southern States of this confederacy. Although each State, as a sovereign political community, must finally determine these grave issues for itself, yet the identity of interests, sympathy, and institutions, prevailing alike in all of the slave-holding States, in the opinion of Alabama renders it proper that there should be a frank and friendly consultation by each one with her sister Southern States touching their common grievances and the measures necessary to be adopted to protect the interest, honor, and safety of their citizens. I come, then, in a spirit of fraternity, as the commissioner on the part of the State of Alabama, to confer with the authorities of this Commonwealth in reference to the infraction of our constitutional rights, wrongs done and threatened to be done, as well as the mode and measure of redress proper to be adopted by the sovereign States aggrieved to preserve their sovereignty, vindicate their rights, and protect their citizens. In order to a clear understanding of the appropriate remedy, it may be proper to consider the rights and duties, both of the State and citizen, under the Federal compact, as well as the wrongs done and threatened. I therefore submit for the consideration of Your Excellency the following propositions, which I hope will command your assent and approval:

[. . .]

3. The Federal Government results from a compact entered into between separate, sovereign, and independent States, called the Constitution of the United States, and amendments thereto, by which these sovereign States delegated certain specific powers to be used by that Government for the common defense and general welfare of all the States and their citizens; and when these powers are abused, or used for the destruction of the rights of any State or its citizens, each State has an equal right to judge for itself as well of the violations and infractions of that instrument as of the mode and measure of redress; and if the interest or safety of her citizens demands it, may resume the powers she had delegated without let or hindrance from the Federal Government or any other power on earth.

4. Each State is bound in good faith to observe and keep on her part all the stipulations and covenants inserted for the benefit of other States in the constitutional compact (the only bond of union by which the several States are bound together), and when persistently violated by one party to the prejudice of her sister States, ceases to be obligatory on the States so aggrieved, and they may rightfully declare the compact broken, the union thereby formed dissolved, and stand upon their original rights as sovereign and independent political communities; and further, that each citizen owes his primary allegiance to the State in which he resides, and hence it is the imperative duty

98

of the State to protect him in the enjoyment of all his constitutional rights, and see to it that they are not denied or withheld from him with impunity by any other State or government.

[. . .]

At the time of the adoption of the Federal Constitution African slavery existed in twelve of the thirteen States. Slaves are recognized both as property and as a basis of political power by the Federal compact, and special provisions are made by that instrument for their protection as property. Under the influences of climate and other causes, slavery has been banished from the Northern States; the slaves themselves have been sent to the Southern States and there sold, and their price gone into the pockets of their former owners at the North. And in the meantime African slavery has not only become one of the fixed domestic institutions of the Southern States, but forms an important element of their political power, and constitutes the most valuable species of their property, worth, according to recent estimates, not less than $4,000,000,000; forming, in fact, the basis upon which rests the prosperity and wealth of most of these States, and supplying the commerce of the world with its richest freights, and furnishing the manufactories of two continents with the raw material, and their operatives with bread. It is upon this gigantic interest, this peculiar institution of the South, that the Northern States and their people have been waging an unrelenting and fanatical war for the last quarter of a century; an institution with which is bound up not only the wealth and prosperity of the Southern people, but their very existence as a political community. This war has been waged in every way that human ingenuity, urged on by fanaticism, could suggest. They attack us through their literature, in their schools, from the hustings, in their legislative halls, through the public press, and even their courts of justice forget the purity of their judicial ermine to strike down the rights of the Southern slave-holder and override every barrier which the Constitution has erected for his protection; and the sacred desk is desecrated to this unholy crusade against our lives, our property, and the constitutional rights guaranteed to us by the compact of our fathers. During all this time the Southern States have freely conceded to the Northern States and the people of those States every right secured to them by the Constitution, and an equal interest in the common territories of the Government; protected the lives and property of their citizens of every kind, when brought within Southern jurisdiction; enforced through their courts, when necessary, every law of Congress passed for the protection of Northern property, and submitted ever since the foundation of the Government, with scarcely a murmur, to the protection of their shipping, manufacturing, and commercial interests, by odious bounties, discriminating tariffs, and unjust navigation laws, passed by the Federal Government to the prejudice and injury of their own citizens.

[. . .]

The same fell spirit, like an unchained demon, has for years swept over the plains of Kansas, leaving death, desolation, and ruin in its track. Nor is this the mere ebullition of a few half-crazy fanatics, as is abundantly apparent from the sympathy manifested all over the North, where, in many places, the tragic death of John Brown, the leader of the raid upon Virginia, who died upon the gallows a condemned felon, is celebrated with public honors, and his name canonized as a martyr to liberty; and many, even of the more conservative papers of the Black Republican school, were accustomed to speak of his murderous attack upon the lives of the unsuspecting citizens of Virginia in a half-sneering and half-apologetic tone. And what has the Federal Government done in the meantime to protect slave property upon the common territories of the Union? Whilst a whole squadron of the American Navy is maintained on the coast of Africa at an enormous expense to enforce the execution of the laws against the slave-trade (and properly, too), and the whole Navy is kept afloat to protect the lives and property of American citizens upon the high seas, not a law has been passed by Congress or an arm raised by the Federal Government to protect the slave property of citizens from Southern States upon the soil of Kansas, the common territory and common property of the citizens of all the States, purchased alike by their common treasure, and held by the Federal Government, as declared by the Supreme Court of the United States, as the trustee for all their citizens; but, upon the contrary, a territorial government, created by Congress and supported out of the common treasury, under the influence and control of emigrant-aid societies and abolition emissaries, is permitted to pass laws excluding and destroying all that species of property within her limits, thus ignoring on the part of the Federal Government one of the fundamental principles of all good governments—the duty to protect the property of the citizen—and wholly refusing to maintain the equal rights of the States and the citizens of the States upon their common territories.

As the last and crowning act of insult and outrage upon the people of the South, the citizens of the Northern States, by overwhelming majorities, on the 6th day of November last, elected Abraham Lincoln and Hannibal Hamlin President and Vice-President of the United States. Whilst it may be admitted that the mere election of any man to the Presidency is not *per se* a sufficient cause for a dissolution of the Union, yet when the issues upon and circumstances under which he was elected are properly appreciated and understood, the question arises whether a due regard to the interest, honor, and safety of their citizens, in view of this and all the other antecedent wrongs and outrages, do not render it the imperative duty of the Southern States to resume the powers they have delegated to the Federal Government and interpose their sovereignty for the protection of their citizens.

[. . .]

If the policy of the Republicans is carried out according to the programme indicated by the leaders of the party, and the South submits, degradation and ruin must overwhelm alike all classes of citizens in the Southern States. The slave-holder and non-slave-holder must ultimately share the same fate; all be degraded to a position of equality with free negroes, stand side by side with them at the polls, and fraternize in all the social relations of life, or else there will be an eternal war of races, desolating the land with blood, and utterly wasting and destroying all the resources of the country. Who can look upon such a picture without a shudder? What Southern man, be he slave-holder or non-slave-holder, can without indignation and horror contemplate the triumph of negro equality, and see his own sons and daughters in the not distant future associating with free negroes upon terms of political and social equality, and the white man stripped by the heaven-daring hand of fanaticism of that title to superiority over the black race which God himself has bestowed?

In the Northern States, where free negroes are so few as to form no appreciable part of the community, in spite of all the legislation for their protection, they still remain a degraded caste, excluded by the ban of society from social association with all but the lowest and most degraded of the white race. But in the South, where in many places the African race largely predominates, and as a consequence the two races would be continually pressing together, amalgamation or the extermination of the one or the other would be inevitable. Can Southern men submit to such degradation and ruin? God forbid that they should.

[. . .]

Will the South give up the institution of slavery and consent that her citizens be stripped of their property, her civilization destroyed, the whole land laid waste by fire and sword? It is impossible. She cannot; she will not. Then why attempt longer to hold together hostile States under the stipulations of a violated Constitution? It is impossible. Disunion is inevitable. Why, then, wait longer for the consummation of a result that must come? Why waste further time in expostulations and appeals to Northern States and their citizens, only to be met, as we have been for years past, by renewed insults and repeated injuries? Will the South be better prepared to meet the emergency when the North shall be strengthened by the admission of the new Territories of Kansas, Nebraska, Washington, Jefferson, Nevada, Idaho, Chippewa, and Arizona as non-slaveholding States, as we are warned from high sources will be done within the next four years, under the administration of Mr. Lincoln? Can the true men at the North ever make a more powerful or successful rally for the preservation of our rights and the Constitution than they did in the last Presidential contest? There is nothing to inspire a hope that they can.

Shall we wait until our enemies shall possess themselves of all the powers of the Government; until abolition judges are on the Supreme Court bench, abolition collectors at every port, and abolition postmasters in every town; secret mail agents traversing the whole land, and a subsidized press established in our midst to demoralize our people? Will we be stronger then or better prepared to meet the struggle, if a struggle must come? No, verily. When that time shall come, well may our adversaries laugh at our folly and deride our impotence. The deliberate judgment of Alabama, as indicated by the joint resolutions of her General Assembly, approved February 24, 1860, is that prudence, patriotism, and loyalty to all the great principles of civil liberty, incorporated in our Constitution and consecrated by the memories of the past, demand that all the Southern States should now resume their delegated powers, maintain the rights, interests, and honor of their citizens, and vindicate their own sovereignty. And she most earnestly but respectfully invites her sister sovereign State, Kentucky, who so gallantly vindicated the sovereignty of the States in 1798, to the consideration of these grave and vital questions, hoping she may concur with the State of Alabama in the conclusions to which she has been driven by the impending dangers that now surround the Southern States.

QUESTIONS

1. What is Hale's critique of northern actions on slavery?
2. What future does he predict under a Republican presidential administration?
3. Why does Hale believe that all the slaveholding states should secede and found a new government?

Source: Published in the United States War Department, *The War of Rebellion: A Compilation of the Official Records of the Union and Confederate Armies*, 127 vols., index, and atlas (Washington: GPO, 1880–1901), Series IV, Volume 1: 4–11.

CHAPTER 14

THE CIVIL WAR, 1860 TO 1865

14.1. CORPORAL WILBUR FISK, EXCERPTS FROM LETTERS TO THE *GREEN MOUNTAIN FREEMAN* (MAY 20, 1862, AND APRIL 7, 1864)

Wilbur Fisk, born and raised in Vermont, enlisted in Company E of the 2nd Vermont Volunteers in 1861. Over the course of the war, Fisk wrote over 100 letters to the Montpelier *Green Mountain Freeman*, his community's newspaper. The first letter below was written in the midst of the failed Union effort to seize Richmond. The second was written at a later point in the war, when the North was experiencing more success.

May 20, 1862

The inevitable negro question would of course be the subject of the most animated conversation of anything we could bring up, for that inexhaustible subject claims preeminence in camp as well as court, and there are almost as many opinions expressed in regard to it in a tent's company as there are in Congress. The boys think it *their* duty to put down rebellion and nothing more, and they view the abolition of slavery in the present time as saddling so much additional labor upon them before the present great work is accomplished. Negro prejudice is as strong here as anywhere and most of the boys would think it a humiliating compromise to the dignity of their work to have it declared that the object of their services was to free the repulsive creatures from slavery, and raise the negro to an equality with themselves. I verily believe if such a declaration was made to-day a majority would be inclined to lay down their arms and quit the service in disgust. The most cordial reception by far that we have received since we left the free states, was tendered us by this sable species of human property. As we were passing by the premises of one of the more wealthy farmers on our way here, a group of negroes, a score or more composed of men, women and children of all ages, climbed upon the fence by the roadside and greeted us in in their earnest simple way "God bress you," "I's glad to see you," "I's glad you's come," "God bress you," and many similar exclamations as they bowed, and courtesied, and waved their hands to us, attesting their childish glee at seeing so many Union soldiers. They were dirty and ragged and probably as a perfectly natural result were ignorant and degraded,

Source: Emil and Ruth Rosenblatt, eds., *Hard Marching Every Day: The Civil War Letters of Private Wilbur Fisk, 1861–1865* (Lawrence: University Press of Kansas, 1983).

but they seemed to understand, as nearly all the ne-groes here do, that somehow all this commotion has a connection with them and will bring about their free-dom in the end. They seem conscious of being at the the bottom of all this trouble, and all the deceptions their masters could invent have failed to rob them of this knowledge. . . .

April 7, 1864

Great confidence is felt in the plans that General Grant will adopt, and the means that he will have to use in crushing the last vestige of this Heaven accursed rebel-lion. Having authority that extends from the Atlantic to the Mississippi from Mobile to Washington, we may reasonably expect a concert of action in the coming campaigns that will ensure us success and victory. God grant that we may not be disappointed.

Success and victory! whose heart does not beat quicker at the thought? What consequences will have been achieved when this great rebellion shall have been forever humbled. It is not merely that this ter-rible war may be ended, and we safely at liberty again, that we hope to conquer our enemies and be once more at peace, but that the great principles of a free government, whose worth no mind short of Infinite Wisdom can estimate, and which even after the world has stood so long is still considered an experiment, may not be overthrown, and the progress of civiliza-tion and freedom may not be rolled back for ages, or receive a blow from which they may never recover. We are anxious of course to get out of this war, for we long most earnestly to return to the almost sacred hills and valleys of old Vermont, but we are not so anxious for this, as we are that the faith of the world in the intelligence and virtue of the common people, and their ability to govern themselves and maintain national unity without being rent asunder by internal strife and discord—a faith that despots the world over profess to sneer at, and hold to be a delusion, and which stimulates the noblest energies of the masses of mankind—that this may be maintained, increased and perpetuated. If these principles succeed, Slavery must fall, and fall forever. The two are so antagonis-tical that, even if both are right, or neither of them, men embracing each could not possibly live together

in peace, unless we are to suppose that God has given them a larger spirit of forbearance than is vouchsafed to humanity in general. There never was a real unity between them, and there never can be. Slavery is a relic of the darkest ages, and the poorest government on earth is better in principle than that. If we are going to have a free government at all, let us have it all free, or else we had better give up the name. Slavery has fos-tered an aristocracy of the rankest kind, and this aris-tocracy is the bitterest foe that a really free government can have. Slavery and despotism have challenged war with us, and by it she must abide. Slavery was jealous of the comelier strength that Freedom possessed; and maliciously envied her irresistible march onward to a higher destiny. Slavery drew the sword, and would have stabbed Freedom to the heart, had not God denied her the strength. She could not bear that her more righteous neighbor should be prospered, while she herself was accursed, and in her foolish madness she has tried to rend the Union in twain. With that in-stitution it is success or death. Compromise with Slav-ery, and restore the Union with Slavery in it still! As well might Jehovah compromise with Satan and give him back part of Heaven.

[. . .]

I almost lose my temper sometimes (what little I have got) when I hear men that really ought to know better, call this war a mere crusade to free the negroes, "a nigger war" and nothing more. But even if I was fighting to free the negroes simply, I don't know why I should be acting from a motive that I need be ashamed of. I verily believe that He who when He was on the earth healed foul leprosy, gave sight to the blind beg-gars, and preached the gospel to the poor, would not be ashamed to act from such a motive. And if he would not, why should I? Fighting to free the "niggers!" Why yes, my dear fellow, we are doing just that and a great deal more. But, sir, I am going to tell you, you would not speak of that so contemptuously, if you had not all your life long fed your soul upon motives so small, so mean, and so selfish, that the sublimer motives of sacrificing blood and treasure to elevate a degraded and downtrodden race, is entirely beyond your com-prehension. Should such an event, however, rather help than hinder the success of this war, we trust that you will acquiesce in the result, and when the future of this country shall have become by this means more glorious than the past has ever been, we shall hope that you will find that your own liberty and happiness has not been at all infringed upon by giving the same liberty and happiness to a few ignorant and despised sons of Africa.

QUESTIONS

1. How does Fisk characterize the attitudes of his fellow soldiers toward blacks and slavery?
2. How does he explain the relationship between slavery and democracy?
3. Why is Fisk fighting the war?

14.2. SPOTSWOOD RICE, LETTERS WRITTEN FROM HOSPITAL (SEPTEMBER 3, 1864)

Spotswood Rice, an enslaved man, worked as a tobacco roller before the Civil War. During the war, he enlisted in the 67th U.S. Colored Infantry. When he wrote the following letters, the first to his children and the second to his daughter's owner, Rice was confined to the hospital with chronic rheumatism.

[Benton Barracks Hospital, St. Louis, Mo.,
September 3, 1864]

My Children   I take my pen in hand to rite you A few lines to let you know that I have not forgot you and that I want to see you as bad as ever   now my Dear Children I want you to be contented with whatever may be your lots   be assured that I will have you if it cost me my life   on the 28th of the mounth. 8 hundred White and 8 hundred blacke solders expects to start up the rivore to Glasgow and above there thats to be jeneraled by a jeneral that will give me both of you   when they Come I expect to be with, them and expect to get you both in return.   Dont be uneasy my children   I expect to have you.   If Diggs dont give you up this Government will and I feel confident that I will get you   Your Miss Kaitty said that I tried to steal you   But I'll let her know that god never intended for man to steal his own flesh and blood.   If I had no confidence in God I could have confidence in her   But as it is If I ever had any Confidence in her I have none now and never expect to have   And I want her to remember if she meets me with ten thousand soldiers she [will?] meet her enemy   I once [thought] that I had some respect for them but now my respects is worn out and have no sympathy for Slaveholders.   And as for her cristianantty I expect the Devil has Such in hell   You tell her from me that She is the frist Christian that I ever hard say that aman could Steal his own child especially out of human bondage

You can tell her that She can hold to you as long as she can   I never would expect to ask her again to let you come to me because I know that the devil has got her hot set against that that is write   now my Dear children I am a going to close my letter to you   Give my love to all enquiring friends   tell them all that

Source: Ira Berlin, Joseph P. Reidy, and Leslie S. Rowland, eds., *Freedom: A Documentary History of Emancipation, 1861–1867,* *Series II: The Black Military Experience* (Cambridge: Cambridge University Press, 1982), 689.

we are well and want to see them very much and Corra and Mary receive the greater part of it you sefves   and dont think hard of us not sending you any thing   I you father have a plenty for you when I see you   Spott & Noah sends their love to both of you   Oh! My Dear children how I do want to see you

HL   [Spotswood Rice]

[Benton Barracks Hospital, St. Louis, Mo., September 3, 1864]

I received a letter from Cariline telling me that you say I tried to steal to plunder my child away from you   now I want you to understand that mary is my Child and she is a God given rite of my own and you may hold on to hear as long as you can but I want you to remember this one thing that the longor you keep my Child from me the longor you will have to burn in hell and the qwicer youll get their   for we are now makeing up a bout one thoughsand blacke troops to Come up tharough and wont to come through Glasgow and when we come wo be to Copperhood rabbels and to the Slave-holding rebbels for we dont expect to leave them there root neor branch   but we thinke how ever that we that have Children in the hands of you devels we will trie your [vertues?] the day that we enter Glasgow   I want you to understand kittey diggs that where ever you and I meets we are enmays to each orthere   I offered once to pay you forty dollers for my own Child but I am glad now that you did not accept it   Just hold on now

as long as you can and the worse it will be for you you never in you life befor I came down hear did you give Children any thing not eny thing whatever not even a dollers worth of expencs   now you call my children your pro[per]ty   not so with me   my Children is my own and I expect to get them and when I get ready to come after mary I will have bout a powrer and autherity to bring hear away and to exacute vengencens on them that holds my Child   you will then know how to talke to me   I will assure that and you will know how to talk rite too   I want you now to just hold on to hear if you want to   iff your conchosence tells that's the road go that road and what it will brig you to kittey diggs   I have no fears about getting mary out of your hands   this whole Government gives chear to me and you cannot helps your self

ALS   Spotswood Rice

QUESTIONS

1. How does Christianity inform Rice's commentary on slavery?
2. How would "Miss Kaitty" have responded to the reversal of power to which Rice refers when he says that he will come to her with ten thousand soldiers?
3. What does Rice's letter tell us about slave families and the relationship between parents and children?

14.3. CATHERINE EDMONSTON, EXCERPTS FROM DIARY (JANUARY 9, 1865)

Catherine Edmonston was a plantation mistress born and raised in North Carolina. During the war, she lived on the Looking Glass Plantation in Halifax County, in the eastern Piedmont. She maintained a detailed diary that was published long after her death. In early 1865, Confederates debated enlisting black men as soldiers into the Confederate Army. Robert E. Lee and Jefferson Davis pushed the measure and it became law, though too late for any black Confederates to take the field. The Confederate Congress refused to authorize emancipation as an incentive for enlistment.

"Out of the abundance of the heart the mouth speaketh," but the hand writeth not. Never were we more absorbed in outward matters, never have we looked on them so anxiously as now, & yet it is days since I have written aught of them. This negro question, this vexed negro question, will if much longer discussed do us more injury than the loss of a battle. Gen Lee advises the Conscription & ultimate Emancipation of 200,000 Slaves to be used as soldiers. One or two rabid partizan papers, Democratic, I might also say Agrarian to the core, seize on the proposal, hold it up to the people, to the army, in the most attractive lights. They promise the white soldier that if the negro is put in the army, for every negro soldier fifteen whites ones will be allowed to return home. They use it as an engine to inflame the passion of one class against another, tell the poor man that the War is but for his rich neighbor's slaves, that his blood is poured out to secure additional riches to the rich, etc., etc., nay one paper, to its shame be it said, the Richmond Enquirer, openly advocates a general Emancipation! as the price for fancied benefits to be obtained by an alliance with England & France. Actually it offers to sell the birthright of the South, not for a mess of pottage, but only for the hope of obtaining one. The Traitor recreant to principle, lost to every sense of national honour, & blind to what constitutes a true national prosperity – the wonder is that he finds anyone either to read or think seriously of his monstrous proposition. But so it is. Coming as it does on the evacuation of Savannah when we are almost ready to sink under the accumulation of Yankee lies & Yankee bragg, over their boated Victory over Hood, our money depreciated & depreciating daily more & more, deafened on one side by loud mouthed politicians who advocate "Reconstruction to save Annihilation," "Reconstruction as a choice of Evils," & on the other by the opponents of the Government who expatiate with alass too much truth upon the mismanagement, the waste, the oppression which, cast our eyes which way we will we see around us, threatened again with a new suspension of Habeas Corpus, the Constitution daily trampled under foot by Impressment Laws & Government Schedules, what wonder that many unthinking people catch at this straw as at hope of salvation & delivery from present misery without pausing to ask themselves what will be their condition when they have accepted it. But sounder & better councils will prevail. This beaten and crushed Abolitionist, the Enquirer, will find that the body of the people are against him, that the foxes who have lost their tails are too few in number to govern those who still retain theirs. Slaveholders on principle,

Source: Catherine Edmondston, *Journal of a Secesh Lady: The Diary of Catherine Ann Devereux Edmondston*, eds. Beth Crabtree and James Patton (Raleigh, N. C.: Division of Archives and History, 1979), 652–653.

& those who hope one day to become slaveholders in their time, will not tacitly yeild their property & their hope & allow a degraded race to be placed at one stroke on a level with them. But these discussions & these thoughts have occupied us for the past fortnight & such a deluge of gloomy forebodings have been penned out upon us that I almost hailed the frequent mail failures as a blessing."

QUESTIONS

1. Why is Edmonston concerned about the debate over slave enlistment in the Confederate armies?
2. What conclusions can we draw from this piece about class relations within the Confederacy?
3. Does Edmonston seem ready to reconcile with the North?

14.4. VISUAL DOCUMENT: ANDREW J. RUSSELL, *RUINS IN RICHMOND* (1865)

After a long siege, the Union Army forced the Confederates to abandon their capital in early April 1865. Before leaving the city, Confederates set fire to material they did want the Union to seize. The fire ran out of control and consumed much of the downtown business district. Andrew Russell worked with the U.S. Military Railroad Construction Corps during the conflict.

Source: Andrew J. Russell, "Ruins in Richmond" April 1865. Library of Congress. Available at: http://www.loc.gov/exhibits/treasures/images/vc46.5.jpg

QUESTIONS

1. What image of war does this photo generate?
2. How would southerners and northerners have explained what happened for the war to reach this level of destructiveness?

3. What lessons does the photo suggest about the costs of war?

14.5. VISUAL DOCUMENT: *ALBANY EVENING JOURNAL*, "GENERAL LEE AND HIS ARMY HAVE SURRENDERED" (APRIL 10, 1865)

After abandoning Richmond, Robert E. Lee's army retreated west until Grant's troops cut them off at Appomattox Courthouse, a small village about 100 miles west of the city. Although one major Confederate army remained in the field (in North Carolina), many Northerners interpreted Lee's defeat as the end of the war.

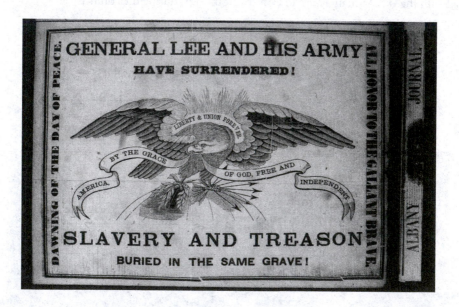

QUESTIONS

1. How does the newspaper explain the purpose and accomplishments of the war?
2. What is the relationship between emancipation and reunion in the announcement?

3. What does the word "treason" suggest about how Confederates might be treated after the war?

Source: Courtesy University of Virginia Periodicals Collections.

CHAPTER 15

RECONSTRUCTING AMERICA, 1865 TO 1877

15.1. JOURDON ANDERSON, LETTER TO P. H. ANDERSON (AUGUST 7, 1865)

Jourdon Anderson was one of the many ex-slaves who made their way north out of Tennessee and Kentucky into southern Ohio after the Civil War. The confused state of the labor market in the South led some masters to try to recruit former slaves back to their property to work as paid laborers.

Dayton, Ohio, August 7, 1865

To My Old Master, Colonel P. H. Anderson, Big Spring, Tennessee

Sir: I got your letter and was glad to find you had not forgotten Jourdon, and that you wanted me to come back and live with you again, promising to do better for me than anybody else can. I have often felt uneasy about you. I thought the Yankees would have hung you long before this for harboring Rebs they found at your house. I suppose they never heard about your going to Col. Martin's to kill the Union soldier that was left by his company in their stable. Although you shot at me twice before I left you, I did not want to hear of your being hurt, and am glad you are still living. It would do me good to go back to the dear old home again and see Miss Mary and Miss Martha and

Allen, Esther, Green, and Lee. Give my love to them all, and tell them I hope we will meet in the better world, if not in this. I would have gone back to see you all when I was working in the Nashville Hospital, but one of the neighbors told me Henry intended to shoot me if he ever got a chance.

I want to know particularly what the good chance is you propose to give me. I am doing tolerably well here; I get $25 a month, with victuals and clothing; have a comfortable home for Mandy (the folks here call her Mrs. Anderson), and the children—Milly, Jane and Grundy—go to school and are learning well; the teacher says Grundy has a head for a preacher. They go to Sunday-School, and Mandy and me attend church regularly. We are kindly treated; sometimes we overhear others saying, "Them colored people were slaves" down in Tennessee. The children feel hurt when they

Source: Lydia Maria Child, *The Freedmen's Book* (Boston: Tickenor and Fields, 1865), 265–67. Also see http://historymatters. gmu.edu/d/6369/.

hear such remarks, but I tell them it was no disgrace in Tennessee to belong to Col. Anderson. Many darkies would have been proud, as I used to be, to call you master. Now, if you will write and say what wages you will give me, I will be better able to decide whether it would be to my advantage to move back again.

As to my freedom, which you say I can have, there is nothing to be gained on that score, as I got my free papers in 1864 from the Provost-Marshal-General of the Department of Nashville. Mandy says she would be afraid to go back without some proof that you are sincerely disposed to treat us justly and kindly; and we have concluded to test your sincerity by asking you to send us our wages for the time we served you. This will make us forget and forgive old scores, and rely on your justice and friendship in the future. I served you faithfully for thirty-two years and Mandy twenty years. At twenty-five dollars a month for me, and two dollars a week for Mandy, our earnings would amount to eleven thousand six hundred and eighty dollars. Add to this the interest for the time our wages has been kept back and deduct what you paid for our clothing and three doctor's visits to me, and pulling a tooth for Mandy, and the balance will show what we are in justice entitled to. Please send the money by Adams Express, in care of V. Winters, Esq., Dayton, Ohio. If you fail to pay us for faithful labors in the past we can have little faith in your promises in the future. We trust the good Maker has opened your eyes to the wrongs which you and your fathers have done to me and my fathers, in making us toil for you for generations without recompense. Here I draw my wages every Saturday night, but in Tennessee there was never any payday for the Negroes any more than for the horses and cows. Surely there will be a day of reckoning for those who defraud the laborer of his hire.

In answering this letter please state if there would be any safety for my Milly and Jane, who are now grown up and both good-looking girls. You know how it was with Matilda and Catherine. I would rather stay here and starve, and die if it comes to that, than have my girls brought to shame by the violence and wickedness of their young masters. You will also please state if there has been any schools opened for the colored children in your neighborhood, the great desire of my life now is to give my children an education, and have them form virtuous habits.

P.S. —Say howdy to George Carter, and thank him for taking the pistol from you when you were shooting at me.

From your old servant,
Jourdon Anderson

QUESTIONS

1. What do Anderson's comments reveal about the economic knowledge of former slaves?
2. What are the attributes of freedom that Anderson identifies as most important?
3. Explain the new power dynamic between Anderson and his former master. How would each of the participants have understood it?

15.2. VISUAL DOCUMENT: THOMAS NAST, ANDREW JOHNSON'S RECONSTRUCTION IN HARPER'S WEEKLY (SEPTEMBER 1, 1866)

During the summer of 1866, Memphis and New Orleans experienced horrible race riots, in which whites murdered dozens of blacks indiscriminately. Many Northerners felt that Johnson's lenient policies fomented a recalcitrant and unapologetic white South. Thomas Nast drew political cartoons for *Harper's Weekly*, the most widely read periodical in the country. He was an early critic of Johnson and a strong proponent for a Reconstruction that treated African Americans fairly.

Source: Ben and Beatrice Goldstein Foundation Collection/Library of Congress.

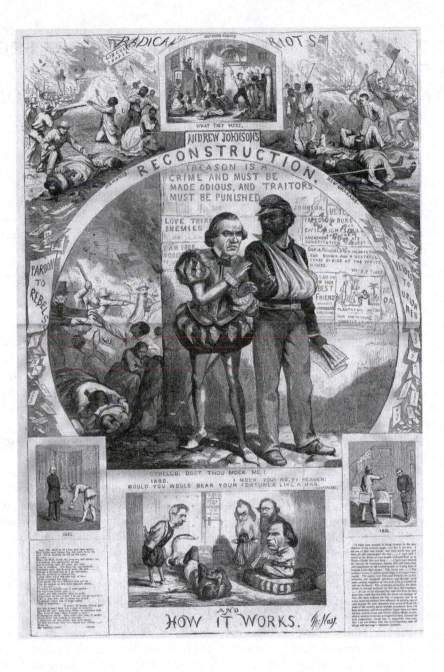

QUESTIONS

1. What is Nast's critique of Johnson's Reconstruction policy?

2. What do the images around the margins of the cartoon portray as Johnson's responsibility for the riots?

3. Why does Nast portray the lone black individual as a wounded Union soldier?

15.3. GEORGES CLEMENCEAU, EXCERPT FROM AMERICAN RECONSTRUCTION, 1865–1870, AND THE IMPEACHMENT OF ANDREW JOHNSON (1867)

By late 1867, Andrew Johnson, a wartime Republican who ascended to the presidency after Lincoln's assassination, had alienated himself from Congressional Republicans because of his conservative approach to Reconstruction. Johnson turned to northern Democrats and southerners (even though many remained disfranchised following the war) for support. Georges Clemenceau, a French physician and journalist, covered Washington politics for a French newspaper. He served as prime minister of France during the last year of World War I and helped draft the Treaty of Versailles.

September 10, 1867. The war between the President and Congress goes on, complicated from time to time by some unexpected turn. Contrary to all that has happened, is happening, and will happen in certain countries, the legislative power here has the upper hand. That is the peculiarity of the situation, or rather of this government. Congress may, when it pleases, take the President by the ear and lead him down from his high seat, and he can do nothing about it except to struggle and shout. But that is an extreme measure, and the radicals are limiting themselves, for the present, to binding Andrew Johnson firmly with good brand-new laws. At each session they add a shackle to his bonds, tighten the bit in a different place, file a claw or draw a tooth, and then when he is well bound up, fastened, and caught in an inextricable net of laws and decrees, more or less contradicting each other, they tie him to the stake of the Constitution and take a good look at him, feeling quite sure he cannot move this time.

But then Seward, the Dalila of the piece, rises up and shouts: "Johnson, here come the radicals with old Stevens at their head; they are proud of having subjected you and are coming to enjoy the sight of you in chains." And Samson summons all his strength, and bursts his cords and bonds with a mighty effort, and the Philistines (I mean the radicals) flee in disorder to the Capitol to set to work making new laws stronger than the old, which will break in their turn at the first test. This has been going on now for two years, and though in the course of things it is inevitable that Samson will be beaten, one must admit that he has put up a game fight. Even a sceptic, if this word has any meaning in America, would be interested in the struggle.

[. . .]

A new amnesty has been proclaimed for the former rebels in the South, and we shall soon see the struggle begin on a new point, that is, the interpretation to be given this proclamation of amnesty and the conclusions to be drawn from it. This is the second proclamation of amnesty which Mr. Johnson has issued. Though it still insists on the obligation to swear the oath of allegiance to the Constitution and the Union, it is infinitely more liberal in its terms than the first proclamation. Instead of the fourteen classes of exceptions defined in the proclamation of amnesty of May 29, 1865, the proclamation of September 8, 1867, defines only three. None are excluded from the benefits of amnesty except the military and civil heads of the Confederate government, those who treated Federal prisoners contrary to the laws of warfare, and those who took

Sources: American Reconstruction, 1865–1870, and the Impeachment of Andrew Johnson, ed. Fernand Baldensperger (New York: Dial Press, 1928), 102–7.

part in the conspiracy which ended in the assassination of Lincoln. The *Tribune* estimated that the first proclamation left about one hundred thousand citizens out of the amnesty, and that this one leaves out one or two thousand. There is no harm done so far, but the question will be what are the exact rights conferred by the amnesty, in other words, whether the President has the power to reinstate the former rebels in their rights and to make voters of them. The President and the Democrats say *Yes*, Congress and the Republicans say *No*.

[. . .]

The Indians in the West have arrayed themselves against the whites, for the thousandth time. Massacres are being carried on by both sides, with brutal ferocity.

The whites hunt down and drive the Indians as they formerly did the negroes in the South, and the Indians, in return, when they take prisoners, send them back to their relatives in pieces, without regard for age or sex. It is sad to be obliged to state that the first and real offenders are nearly always the white men.

QUESTIONS

1. How does Clemenceau characterize relations between the president and Congress?
2. How would Johnson's more liberal amnesty rules affect the landscape of postwar politics?
3. What connections were there between the Indian wars of the West and the Civil War?

15.4. KU KLUX KLAN, LETTER TO MRS. I. A. BALDWIN (1868)

Founded in 1866, the Ku Klux Klan was a terrorist organization devoted to driving black people out of positions of public authority in the South. Its members operated in secret and used all manner of threats and violence to break the political alliances between blacks and whites in the Republican Party and the social institutions built by black Southerners in the postwar years.

Notice has been sent to Mrs. L. A. Baldwin, teacher of freedmen's school No. 1, Bowling Green, Kentucky, with post office dated April 27, 1868, of which the following is a copy.

Mrs. L. A. Baldwin, teacher colored school, Bowling Green, Kentucky:

KU KLUX KLANS!
BLOOD! POISON! POWDER! TORCH!
Leave in five days, or hell's your portion!
Rally, rally, watch your chance,
First blood, first premium K. K. K.
If ball, or torch, or poison fails,

The house beneath you shall be blown to hell, or move you.

K. K. K.

QUESTIONS

1. Why would the KKK attack teachers?
2. What threat did education pose to the social order?
3. How would the anonymous nature of the threat delivered to Mrs. L. A. Baldwin affect the social fabric of the Kentucky community in which she lived?

Source: Secretary of War, House Executive Document No. 329, 40th Cong., 2nd sess., 19.

15.5. NORTH CAROLINA SHARECROPPING CONTRACT (JULY 21, 1882)

Beginning in 1865, freedpeople signed labor agreements with former plantation owners to share the growth and harvesting of cotton. Landholders granted access to the land and sharecroppers provided labor. Although sharecropping initially met the complementary needs of white and black Southerners in the first days of Reconstruction, the contracts exploited the landlessness of black Southerners and created a crisis of debt that trapped many farming families.

To every one applying to rent land upon shares, the following conditions must be read, and agreed to. To every 30 and 35 acres, I agree to furnish the team, plow, and farming implements, except cotton planters, and I do not agree to furnish a cart to every cropper. The croppers are to have half of the cotton, corn, and fodder (and peas and pumpkins and potatoes if any are planted) if the following conditions are complied with, but — if not — they are to have only two-fifths (2/5). Croppers are to have no part or interest in the cotton seed raised from the crop planted and worked by them. No vine crops of any description, that is, no watermelons, muskmelons,… squashes or anything of that kind, except peas and pumpkins, and potatoes, are to be planted in the cotton or corn. All must work under my direction. All plantation work to be done by the croppers. My part of the crop to be housed by them, and the fodder and oats to be hauled and put in the house. All the cotton must be topped about 1st August. If any cropper fails from any cause to save all the fodder from his crop, I am to have enough fodder to make it equal to one-half of the whole if the whole amount of fodder had been saved.

For every mule or horse furnished by me there must be 1000 good sized rails… hauled, and the fence repaired as far as they will go, the fence to be torn down and put up from the bottom if I so direct. All croppers to haul rails and work on fence whenever I may order. Rails to be split when I may say. Each cropper to clean out every ditch in his crop, and where a ditch runs between two croppers, the cleaning out of that ditch is to be divided equally between them. Every ditch bank in the crop must be shrubbed down and cleaned off before the crop is planted and must be cut down every time the land is worked with his hoe and when the crop is "laid by," the ditch banks must be left clean of bushes, weeds, and seeds. The cleaning out of all ditches must be done by the first of October. The rails must be split and the fence repaired before corn is planted.

[. . .]

All croppers must clean out stable and fill them with straw, and haul straw in front of stable whenever I direct. All the cotton must be manured, and enough fertilizer must be brought to manure each crop highly, the croppers to pay for one-half of all manure bought, the quantity to be purchased for each crop must be left to me.

No cropper is to work off the plantation when there is any work to be done on the land he has rented, or when his work is needed by me or other croppers. Trees to be cut down on Orchard, house field, & Evanson fences, leaving such as I may designate.

Road field is to be planted from the very edge of the ditch to the fence, and all the land to be planted close up to the ditches and fences. No stock of any

Source: Grimes Family Papers (#3357), 1882, in the Southern Historical Collection, University of North Carolina at Chapel Hill. Available at: http://www.learnnc.org/lp/editions/nchist-newsouth/4765.

kind belonging to croppers to run in the plantation after crops are gathered.

[. . .]

Every cropper must feed or have fed, the team he works, Saturday nights, Sundays, and every morning before going to work, beginning to feed his team (morning, noon, and night every day in the week) on the day he rents and feeding it to including the 31st day of December. If any cropper shall from any cause fail to repair his fence as far as 1000 rails will go, or shall fail to clean out any part of his ditches, or shall fail to leave his ditch banks, any part of them, well shrubbed and clean when his crop is laid by, or shall fail to clean out stables, fill them up and haul straw in front of them whenever he is told, he shall have only two-fifths (2/5) of the cotton, corn, fodder, peas, and pumpkins made on the land he cultivates.

[. . .]

Every cropper must be responsible for all gear and farming implements placed in his hands, and if not returned must be paid for unless it is worn out by use.

Croppers must sow & plow in oats and haul them to the crib, but must have no part of them. Nothing to be sold from their crops, nor fodder nor corn to be carried out of the fields until my rent is all paid, and all amounts they owe me and for which I am responsible are paid in full.

I am to gin & pack all the cotton and charge every cropper an eighteenth of his part, the cropper to furnish his part of the bagging, ties, & twine.

The sale of every cropper's part of the cotton to be made by me when and where I choose to sell, and after deducting all they owe me and all sums that I may be responsible for on their accounts, to pay them their half of the net proceeds. Work of every description, particularly the work on fences and ditches, to be done to my satisfaction, and must be done over until I am satisfied that it is done as it should be.

QUESTIONS

1. Why did the contract prohibit the growing garden crops (watermelons, squash, etc.) on the land?
2. Why did the landholder claim the sole authority to sell whatever cotton was raised?
3. In what ways could sharecropping produce unexpected results for the sharecroppers?

CPSIA information can be obtained
at www.ICGtesting.com
Printed in the USA
FSOW04n1550160917
38721FS